# Ian Ritchie

Ian Ritchie
**Technoecology**

text by Alessandro Rocca

**Whitney Library of Design**
An imprint of Watson-Guptill Publications/New York

*Cover:* Detail, stainless steel mesh and
stone fill wall, Experimental Greenhouse,
Terrasson-Lavilledieu, France
(Photograph by Jocelyne Van den Bossche)

First printed in the United States by Whitney Library
of Design, an imprint of Watson-Guptill Publications,
a division of BPI Communications, Inc.,
1515 Broadway, New York, NY, 10036.

© 1998 Federico Motta Editore SpA
© 1998 Whitney Library of Design, English language edition

Original Title: Ian Ritchie: *Tecnoecologia*

*Direction*
Pierluigi Nicolin

*Editorial Supervision*
Guia Sambonet

*Graphic Design*
Giorgio Camuffo/Gaetano Cassini

Translated from the Italian by Judyth Schaubhut Smith

Library of Congress Catalog Card Number: 98-86725.
ISBN 0-8230-2508

Manufactured in Italy
First U.S. printing, 1998

# Ian Ritchie: Technoecology

*Alessandro Rocca*

After receiving a degree in architecture in 1972, Ian Ritchie joined the firm of Norman Foster and Michael Hopkins, where he collaborated on the Willis, Faber & Dumas office building in Ipswich. In England, these were the transitional years that would eventually dismantle the apparatus of radical Modernism and its utopian polemics in favor of the new wave of High-Tech architecture, as witnessed by the Ipswich project itself. Still under the influence of the Archigram movement while pursuing his studies, Ritchie (whose thesis advisor was Warren Chalk) had presented an audiovisual display on future land use for leisure-time activities in an urban environment. However, as soon as he became a member of Foster's team, where he had occasion to work with the aging Jean Prouvé, he was exposed to the various themes involved in technical research. He also established important working relationships with Martin Francis and Anthony Hunt, the latter a structural engineer who would become a leading figure on the British architectural scene.

Ritchie's first commission, Fluy House, reflected both his personal experience and the new spirit of the times. Set in the countryside of Piccardy, this single-story structure was designed and built from 1976 to 1978 for the parents of his female companion, Jocelyn Van den Bossche. Small, lightweight, and composed of thin-walled hollow steel sections, glass-skinned walls, and aluminum frames and curtains, the house was also equipped with solar energy panels. By reducing the structural elements to an absolute minimum and arranging them in a precise geometric pattern, Ritchie had achieved his goal of utmost economy.

Defined by steel rather than wood, and glass rather than the surrounding landscape, Fluy House was also devoid of any of the expressive details traditionally associated with transparency. As such, it embodied the natural technological evolution of the original cottage. The interior, with its lack of doors and plain, simple, post-Miesian dividing walls, as well as the sobriety of materials and decorative elements used, was reminiscent of the intimate atmosphere of Charles Eames's Modernistic California home.

Ritchie's technology had adopted a colloquial tone as the ultimate means of simplification. In fact, his "railroad flat" design was the antithesis of the ponderous, aristocratic crystal "pavilions" represented by Mies's Farnsworth House, or its replica in New Canaan by Philip Johnson. Rather, it called to mind the house built in Wimbledon by Richard Rogers for his own parents some 10 years earlier (1968-69). In this first commission, Ritchie had already fully revealed the principles that would continue to guide his work, founded on developing technology and the absence of stylized architectural motifs.

For his second commission (1981-82), Eagle Rock House, a spectacular construction located in the countryside of Sussex, Ritchie's search for new technological solutions was enhanced by his need to make a clear architectural statement. In fact, the main living space and two wings, which suggested the body of an eagle (Eagle Rock), were supported by an imposing steel canopy. Once again,

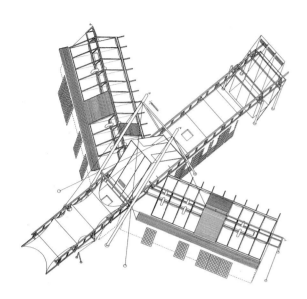

Eagle Rock, Sussex

although on a much reduced scale, Ritchie seemed to have taken his inspiration from Richard Rogers, whose projects at the time, including industrial facilities at Quimper (1979-81), Newport (1982), and Princeton (1982-85), involved the systematic use of structures anchored to aerial steel frames.

Over the years, however, fundamental differences in their approach would become more and more evident. Whereas Rogers increasingly sought to utilize structural elements in a more expressive way, Ritchie was moving in the opposite direction. Having abandoned the idiosyncrasies of Eagle Rock House, he chose to concentrate on the study of materials and transparent surfaces in a constant effort to achieve "more from less," by utilizing the simplicity and economy of a limited number of recurring elements.

**Radical Architecture.** In Ritchie's early commissions, there were still traces of the "Archigram Syndrome" and its concept of "flinging down" a structure as an instantaneous, temporary act. The idea of architectural "installations" that do not interfere with the stability of the original landscape was also inspired by Archigram, as was the aesthetic of a functionalism defined in terms of primary needs, as opposed to the Modernist formalism that the movement had so clearly rejected. "We have chosen to bypass the decaying Bauhaus image, which is an insult to functionalism,"[1] wrote David Greene, followed by Peter Cook, whose assertion that "the prepackaged frozen lunch is more important than Palladio"[2] echoed the words of Marinetti.

In any case, after the era of capsule dwellings and relocatable prefabricated buildings (Warren Chalk's Gasket Houses) came a complete change in the approach to designing and assembling industrial components. For Chalk and Ron Herron, individual dwellings had been considered an integral part of the architecture of a visionary mobile urban environment, Plug-in-City, according to a progression in scale (individual dwelling–building–city) that reflected, in an avant-garde sense, the modern orthodoxy. Ritchie's residential units represented the next generation, in which the relationship between industry and a consumer society—both the fetish and target of Archigram propaganda—was redefined in terms of the design requirements of a particular situation and the actual building process.

Curiously enough, 20 years after Plug-in-City, it was Peter Cook who introduced the world at large to Eagle Rock. In his article, which included a detailed analysis of the house, Cook not only placed Ritchie in the forefront of High-Tech, but also noted that the friction between design and technique had at last been overcome, thus marking the end of the radical utopian movement: "The eagle has at last landed, with all his arrogance and bite. Perhaps the Victorians might have created him—if they had had the technology. They would have enjoyed the possibilities of tension wires and solar panels, of sleek fitting aluminium. They would have enjoyed the sheer theatre of the site and its curious inhabitant. They would have recognised Ritchie as one of themselves: confident in the achievement of industry and knowledgeable of several of its tricks, but too ambitious and witty to let the house sit as a mere playing-out of an admired formula. He is hopefully one of the

1  David Greene, *Archigram*, no. 1, 1961, p. 2.
2  Peter Cook, "Amazing Archigram: Some Rules on the Archigram Syndrome," *Perspecta: The Yale Architectural Journal,* Supplement no. 11, 1967, p. 133.

Experimental greenhouse at La Villette Park, Paris

3  Peter Cook, "Ian Ritchie Takes Flight at Eagle
   Rock," *The Architects' Journal*, no. 43, vol.
   178, October 26, 1983, p. 74.
4  Interview with Ian Ritchie by author.
5  For a more detailed discussion of the life and
   works of Peter Rice, see Alessandro Rocca,
   "Peter Rice, poeta del brutalismo," *Lotus
   International*, no. 78, October 1993, pp. 6-12.
6  The technique of structural glass, which
   immediately rendered the majority of
   construction designs using glass walls obsolete,
   was rapidly adopted in all of Europe. These
   results are best illustrated by the system's
   inventors, Peter Rice and Hugh Dutton, in *Le
   verre structurel*, Paris: Éditions du Moniteur,
   1990.

first architects of a new English house who is enthusiastic enough to show how it can be done, arrogant enough to keep arguing, and talented enough to make a house with that elusive image—quality—of which we should not be frightened."[3]

**Peter Rice, Martin Francis, and Ian Ritchie (RFR).** "In 1981 Peter Rice asked me if I was interested in joining him, as he had been approached by the French government to help on the design of the new Museum of Science, Technology and Industry at La Villette. The design competition had been won by Adrien Fainsilber. I suggested that Martin Francis should join us, as he now lived in France, designing yachts, and would be able to bring an extra expertise—industrial design—to the project. Peter was not keen to do the 'structural steelwork' of the project, but was interested in investigating glass. Peter had never met Martin, so we had supper in Paris together. Rice Francis Ritchie, a design engineering practice, was formed on an equal basis among the three of us during that first meal. I felt particularly indebted to Peter at the time, since I was very much the youngster—34."[4] Ian Ritchie's account explains how the RFR studio—a kind of small pirate ship—was conceived. As such, it allowed Peter Rice a certain amount of freedom from his administrative responsibilities at the most prestigious engineering firm in the world, Ove Arup & Partners of London.

Rice is an extraordinary figure who, in his occasionally ambiguous role as engineer, has exercised an enormous influence over a great many of the most important projects of the past 30 years.[5] After joining Ove Arup in 1956, his first important assignment was the Sydney Opera House, designed by Jørn Utzon, where he was in charge of construction for seven years. He then gained an international reputation with the Centre Pompidou, which marked the beginning of a constant collaboration with Richard Rogers, and above all with Renzo Piano, who involved him in all of his most important projects, and with whom, for a brief period, he formed the Piano & Rice design studio.

In fact, Rice co-authored many of the most significant architectural projects in recent decades. He worked with Norman Foster and I. M. Pei, as well as Kenzo Tange, Oriol Bohigas, Christoph Langhof, Zaha Hadid, Kisho Kurokawa, and Bernard Tschumi. In Paris he was involved in the design of the Grande Arche in La Défense, the Bastille Opera House, La Villette Park, and various projects connected with the renovation of the Louvre.

Rice's interest in experimentation and research into new materials was given new impetus when the RFR studio received its first commission, the experimental greenhouse at the Science and Technology Museum in La Villette. Rice, who along with Ritchie and Francis had been studying the static and technological possibilities of the glass wall, developed a new construction technique, known as "structural glass."[6] This system, which was based on the resistance of glass to the force of traction, developed a method by which each panel became an autonomous structural entity, balanced by the network of tensors. In this way, the loading-bearing framework sustained only the weight of the panels, without having to absorb the sum of all the tensions, as is the case of the "curtain

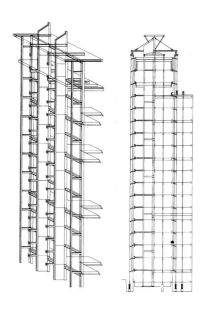

wall." The result was the perfect continuity and transparency of the glass surface, supported by a system of great technical and formal elegance, achieved by anchoring and subjecting to tension each separate panel. The possibilities of structural glass developed by RFR were subsequently used in many other projects in Paris, including the Louvre (I.M. Pei's pyramid and the roofing for the courtyards of the Richelieu wing), Patrick Berger's glasshouses for André Citroën Park, the great transparent roof over Jean-Pierre Buffi's "Collines" at La Défense, and the main offices of the BPOA Bank in Montgermont, designed by Odile Decq and Benoît Cornette.

**Rice's Legacy: Lightness, Transparency, and Immateriality**. From his partnership in RFR, which he abandoned in 1989, Ian Ritchie gained extraordinary technical skills that led to important new projects. After his prolonged immersion in engineering, his return to architecture involved the construction of the B8 Building at Stockley Park, an industrial complex located near London's Heathrow Airport. In designing this office/research facility, Ritchie took the two basic concepts of High-Tech—lightness and transparency—to the ultimate extreme by employing a radical technological approach that was meant to visually "dissolve" the building's architectural structure. His design, which was inspired by Renzo Piano's construction for the Menil Collection in Houston, was that of a homogeneous space dominated by the continuous line of the overhanging roof, allowing for the filtration of light, and acting as a skylight for the internal surfaces and a *brise-soleil* for the external surfaces.

In Piano's building, the space, which was covered with wooden lists, was opaque, and the roof (designed by Peter Rice) was a complex, voluminous structure that produced an extremely plastic effect. In the B8 Building, the walls were entirely substituted by glass curtains with varying degrees of transparency and coloration, while the skylight roof was composed of a thin metallic framework covered with perforated sheets of aluminum, all of which gave the impression of a total absence of weight, or materiality. In this latest experiment, Ritchie went beyond the limits of High-Tech, leaving to others the task of demonstrating that a house—or a city—made of glass and steel can emerge from the dreams of the engineer to become a living reality.

Ritchie's next commission, which followed shortly thereafter, was the design of circulation towers for the Reina Sofia Museum of Modern Art in Madrid. Here, he further developed the technology of structural glass by emphasizing the relationship with the 18th-century building in terms of the contrast between architecture and engineering, heaviness *(gravitas)* and lightness *(levitas),* the volumetric and expressive plasticity of the walls, and the neutrality of the transparent filigree of the glass surfaces.

Originally, Ritchie was asked by the German architectural firm of Von Gerkan, Marg and Partners to assist in the structural engineering of the glass exhibition hall that was to be the centerpiece of the new trade-fair complex in Leipzig. In the end, he was invited to provide the design for the entire building. His

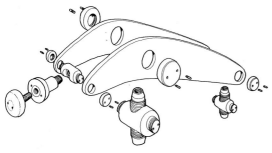

Reina Sofia Museum of Modern Art, Madrid

extraordinary structure, which demonstrated to what extent he considered himself the rightful heir of Peter Rice, was perhaps the most spectacular reinterpretation of the 19th-century theme of the transparent barrel-vaulted gallery.

**Technology As Spectacle.** As Ritchie began to take on the various challenges represented by high technology, he ignored the common vernacular and demagogic concessions employed by many of his colleagues, choosing instead to become part of the extremist wing of the so-called British High-Tech architecture. Thanks to a strict methodology and broad-ranging knowledge of structural engineering, he was able to create technical *tours de force* in their purest form. After his initial projects involving structural glass, he began to experiment with other possibilities, such as coefficients of transparency of treated glass (the office/research facility at Stockley Park), translucent, interactive surfaces (the Greenwich Planetarium), and transmission of light and its ability to transform a building through the use of sophisticated lighting equipment (the monument at Dubai). The technological opportunities offered by glass and light, both natural and artificial, were the basis for his spectacular architectural structures, many of which were further dramatized by the use of elementary geometric forms: circles (the Greenwich Planetarium and Dubai), pure volumes (the towers of Reina Sofia and the B8 Building), perfect planes (which were also transparent in most of his projects), and gigantic vaulted surfaces (the Leipzig Exhibition Center).

**Ritchie and the Others: High-Tech.** As is the case in a number of other European countries, a conflict has again arisen between British Modernists and traditionalists, pitting those who support the avant-garde against those who choose to defend conservation and the reaffirmation of the architectural values of the past. The situation in Great Britain, however, is marked by the radical nature of these opposing forces: on the one hand, High-Tech, with its passionate advocates, and on the other, a traditionalist opposition that continues to focus on the insensitivity and violence of building construction of the 1960s, most probably identifying the medium of concrete—an old but ever-menacing enemy—as its main antagonist. As Robert Maxwell wrote, "...there appear to be only two visible positions: on the one hand, the High-Tech school advocates technical innovation and the use of new materials and methods that may involve risk and can be seen as progressive. Architecture should be something up-to-date, state-of-the-art, equal to the modern world of lasers and computers. This approach is well-received in Britain, and the High-Tech school is replete with knights and beloved of the Establishment. On the other hand, the Prince of Wales has championed the cause of a traditional architecture that works because it follows well-tried and tested ways and avoids unnecessary risk altogether. In both cases, it is the practical argument that is emphasised and personal expression that is played down."[7]

Notwithstanding the amount of support enjoyed by Prince Charles, it is clearly in the area of high technology that English architects have achieved international renown for their extraordinary achievements. It is also interesting to note that

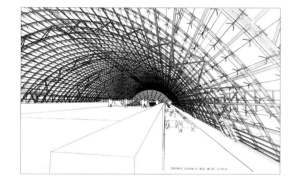

Leipzig International Exhibition Center

7  Robert Maxwell, "Architecture as Art: Transatlantic Parallels," *Contemporary British Architects*, Munich and New York: Prestel, and London: Royal Academy of the Arts, 1994, p. 19.

at a time when other theories and tendencies are losing ground, the High-Tech movement is stronger than ever, and better equipped for success. Thanks to the impasse reached by the rationalist Le Corbusier school, it is now considered the most authoritative among the proponents of Modernist architecture. However, as Maxwell has pointed out, the conspicuous lack of opposing viewpoints within the movement, which represents an attempt to offer the public a simplified version of the final product, has created a gilded cage that limits both freedom of invention and theoretical debate.

In 1981, when Norman Foster was asked to describe his feelings about technology, he stated: "For me the history of gliders is exemplary: over the course of time they have become faster, safer, more comfortable, and much more beautiful; they can cover ever greater distances, use less and less energy...keep up with the most advanced technologies, and give the pilot infinite pleasure."[8] Ideas such as these give us a glimmer of the lesser-known side of the fascination with technology: The modern world, which has run the gamut from the 19th-century myth of technical and scientific progress to recent attempts to reconcile mankind with nature, is once again in search of a new direction. The quest for the immaterial is nearing the end, as are the radical avant-garde (especially Archigram), the notion of the "intelligent building,"[9] and all of our post-industrial and neo-ecological illusions.

Norman Foster's statement reverberates with the echo of a circular pattern that Brian Hatton has described as a "tract with no topography but a mutable semiography."[10] Having freed us from the waste products of blast furnaces and the noise of the internal-combustion engine, the new technologies have awakened a longing for the primordial past. The need to return to one's roots, the fascination with certain primal sites, the lure of a pre-industrial existence, and the adoption of a nomadic lifestyle (whether real or imagined), all of which represent a relief from a restless and unreal media-milieu, are now the myths that are fueling the energy and consensus surrounding high technology.[11]

On the British scene, Ritchie continues to be an integral part of the High-Tech movement, concentrating his efforts on technological experimentation to improve the performance of both structures and materials. While he has obviously shared the mythology of transparency and lightness with Norman Foster, he has also distanced himself from the mechanistic expressionism of Richard Rogers and the numerous mannerisms associated with the work of architects such as Michael Hopkins or Jeremy Dixon.

Instead, Ritchie has found a kindred spirit in Renzo Piano, whose technology is also based on a human scale, and who views his projects as a civic duty, or "service" to humanity. However, the two men's backgrounds are very different: Piano comes from a Mediterranean world in which technology is more "gentle," or softened, by its dialogue with the cultural and social milieu. Ritchie's position, while clearly reflecting a strong identity of his own, has developed in a typically British cultural environment whose main approach Robert Maxwell described as follows: "It is not that High-Tech architecture

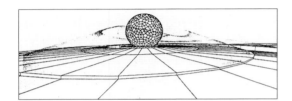

Pearl of the Gulf, Dubai

8  Patrice Goulet, "De l'apparence à la transparence," *L'Architecture d'aujourd'hui*, no. 237, February 1985, pp. LIX-LX.
9  Brian Hatton, "Interview with John Frazer," *Lotus International*, no. 79, December 1993, pp. 15-25.
10 Brian Hatton, "De Re/Media," *Lotus International*, no. 75, February 1993, p. 115.
11 Ibid., pp. 114-16.

Ecology Gallery, London

denies beauty; but beauty must be identified with necessity, as a consequence of applying reason to the principles of engineering. The resulting order must not be based on convention, but on nature; and to be true, this order must lend itself not to the rules of human perception but to the laws of natural perception. In some way, architecture must be protected from any doubts regarding purely aesthetic intentions."[12]

**The Ecology Gallery.** Ritchie has always pursued his own course in a highly original way, developing concepts and ideas that are often outside the mainstream of British High-Tech architecture. The formalism of his early years, especially as embodied in the small structures at Eagle Rock and Boves, soon gave way to a period of technical experimentation with Peter Rice, when the two men concentrated on "forcing" different materials to their utmost limits of performance. The towers at Reina Sofia, and even more dramatically, the B8 Building at Stockley Park, represented a crisis of confidence in the autonomy of architectural form, during which time Ritchie sought refuge in pure tectonics supported by technological innovation. At the end of the 1980s, however, he found the solution to this impasse, once again championing the causes of ecology and environmental control that had been important factors in his first project at Fluy House.
The commission that marked Ritchie's heightened awareness of the importance of emphasizing man's current relationship to the environment was the design and construction of the Ecology Gallery at the Natural History Museum in London, a semi-permanent installation with a planned lifespan of 10 years. In this sophisticated ensemble, he succeeded in communicating his ideas in a simple, direct fashion, without sacrificing any of his technical and figurative prerogatives, and without looking for shortcuts by resorting to the sensationalism of the numerous special effects found in other parts of the museum.
Ritchie's primary objective in designing the gallery was an attempt to emphasize the importance of ecology through expressions of love and respect for the planet Earth. This was achieved by inviting the visitor to observe and understand the life cycle of plants and animals, the ecosystems of arid zones, the biological life of oceans, and many other aspects of the environment. This theme was reinforced in various ways, ranging from the most traditional scenotechnical expedients to the most advanced computerized displays, all within a context offset by irony and surprising figurative allusions.
The stops and starts of the Earth's natural state of disequilibrium are symbolized by subtle devices such as thresholds, steps, narrow paths, and sudden changes in light. Visitors enter the gallery directly from the central atrium of the museum. After crossing a steel threshold in the form of a small Japanese bridge, they find themselves in a long, rectangular space defined by two walls, one vertical and the other convex, which are retroilluminated by opaline glass. Although the overall effect is vaguely science fictional, with a rather cold atmosphere, the three blue bridges that cross this chasm, each on a different plane, as well as nautical details and a structure in the form of a spinal column, lend a

12 Robert Maxwell, "Richard Rogers e la macchina spaziale," *Casabella,* no. 611, April 1994, p. 18.

joyous note to the whole as they "play" with the magniloquence of the vaults above. The path then leads up to the darkened room of the quadrisphere, where special mirrors project 360-degree images of the world's oceans, and finally takes the visitor through various sections highlighted by passageways that cross over the gallery on the floor below.

**Industrial Production and Design.** When confronted with the products on display at the 1851 Crystal Palace Exposition, Gottfried Semper wrote: "Science never ceases to enrich itself and human existence through the discovery of new and useful materials and natural resources that can bring about miracles, with new methods and techniques, with new instruments and machines. At this point it is evident that inventions are no longer, as they once were, a means of meeting needs and fulfilling desires; on the contrary, needs and desires are now the means by which to sell inventions. The natural order of things has been over-turned…. Machines can sew, knit, embroider, carve, paint, invade the territory of manmade art, and put every human endeavor to shame…. The abundance of means is the first serious threat that art must face. Such an expression is in reality a paradox (there is not an abundance of means, but rather an inability to control them), but for this very reason it is justified, because it accurately describes the absurdities of our situation."[13]

Such considerations reflect how difficult it is to function in a world where "the natural order of things has been overturned," where we are unable to control "the abundance of means," and where the products of industry dictate the needs and desires of modern man. For Ritchie, regaining creative control of means of production is the only way to fight against the current that has swept the designer to the end of the industrial chain.

Naturally, in terms of high technology, Ritchie's own theories and arguments have been primarily concerned with the field of "industrial design." As such, they have confronted the issues involved in a century-old debate, which is not only British, on the relationship between art and industry: "Today, in the con-struction industry, after decades dominated by the power of industrial produc-tion of monotonous products resulting from management and manufacturing methods seeking ever more economies, there is now a need to inject art into industry. The design, engineering and manufacture of primary materials into products which carry the signature of the designer, the presence of the human hand, mind and heart, have become essential in order that industry not only serves man's material needs, but also his sensibilities."[14] Once again, accord-ing to Ritchie: "An architecture which uses materials to reflect the condition of society, where these materials are used in their primary state rather than as products, e.g. metal sheet coil, and engages craftsmen to manipulate them, with or without the use of computers, in the factory or in their site assembly, can represent a late 20th-century evolution of the Arts and Crafts tradition."[15] It is primarily with regard to the construction industry that Ritchie has fought such a hard battle against the negative effects of underestimating the impor-

Experimental greenhouse at Terrasson

13  Gottfried Semper, *Wissenschaft, Industrie und Kunst,* Mainz: Florian Kupferlerg Verlag, 1966, pp. 31-32.
14  Ian Ritchie, *(Well) Connected Architecture,* London: Academy Editions, 1994, p. 52.
15  Ibid., pp. 52-53.

tance of industrial design, which has traditionally been allocated a subordinate position with respect to productivity requirements, as well as political and economic priorities. Ritchie's argument, like that of Semper when he was confronted with the deluge of merchandise exhibited at the Crystal Palace, is against kitsch, the vulgarity of technological rhetoric, the approximative and improper use of symbology, and a society that is violated by its acceptance of the rules imposed by a totalitarian technical culture.[16]

In contrast to the climate of indifference and economic exploitation that has characterized so much of modern construction, Ian Ritchie's concern with the environment is first and foremost a moral statement, calling for a return to clarity and coherence through the deliberate choice of the qualities and values that a particular project is meant to communicate. This emphasis on a new morality, which is evident in both his writings and numerous interviews, is based on technological integralism—the need to go beyond performance limitations by introducing a radical revision of design and construction modalities.

In such an endeavor, the main obstacles that lie ahead are not only the pop-become-trash of McDonald's, Disneyworld, television, and the print media, but also mass consumption, which encompasses a system of symbols, values, and tastes that have generated the polyformous universe of contemporary kitsch, whereby authentic industrial design and techniques have been consigned to the limbo of the superfluous and the residual. In response to the vulgarity of today's consumer society, certain industrial designers have attempted a dialogue with the masses in viewing cultural hybridization with a strong sense of irony, while others, as Robert Maxwell has noted in discussing the leading proponents of high technology, have opted to become a part of the system.

**Technoecology.** As of the end of the 1980s, technical research is no longer aimed at the two classic objectives of High-Tech architecture, lightness and transparency. In a recent series of articles and lectures, Ritchie has begun to stress the need for a reevaluation of the relationships between industrial production, architectural design, and the environment in his search for new connections between energy sources and construction techniques, especially with regard to economic factors and environmental conditions. As his own ideological approach to architecture has become increasingly involved in ecological issues, his statements have proved to be both provocative and highly politicized.

Ritchie's Ecology Gallery project not only reinforced his awareness of environmental issues; it also taught him how powerful and persuasive an alternative solution can be when it is no longer intended as merely a technical *tour de force,* but rather a reflection of politics and participation.

The greenhouse at Terrasson, where Ritchie first applied these new concepts, is almost an extension of the landscape. Its feeling of spaciousness comes from the juxtaposition of only a few simple structural elements: the gabion wall and metallic mesh, the glass sheeting of the roof, and a small amphitheater carved out of the earth. In the end, the building is defined by the opposing textures of

Proposed design for Herne-Sodingen Academy, Emscher Park, Germany

16  For a more detailed discussion of this issue, see the introductory chapters of *(Well) Connected Architecture.*

two elements, the crudeness of the rock wall and the precision of the glass roof. Through exploiting the irregular geometry of the site, he has created a sheltered space that becomes one with the hills, the ecology, and the colors of the park. Naturally, at the heart of the project is the technological performance of the clear glass roof, which literally emerges from the landscape, in a constant interplay between lightness and heaviness, opacity and transparency, and primitive elements (the wall and stone amphitheater) and advanced technology.

Ritchie's proposal for the Herne-Sodingen Academy Park, which was to be part of an ambitious land reclamation project along the Ems River Valley in western Germany (Emscher Park), was a far more explicit and radical expression of his concern for the environment than Terrasson had been. Although the project was never realized, it is included in this book because the overall concept, energy schemes, and architectural design can be seen as a manifesto on ecological architecture. This project, which involved the transformation of an industrial and mining area into an academic campus, was developed with two primary objectives in mind: on the one hand, the reclamation and conservation of the land through the intelligent use of available resources (solar energy, wind-driven water pumps, methane gas, and site water sources) to create optimal conditions for the natural environment; on the other, the addition of an artificial valley of glass, concrete, and steel to demonstrate the possibilities offered by ecologically sound architectural design.

For Terrasson and Sodingen, the main problem was the relationship between building materials and the immediate environment. As both projects concerned parklands, Ritchie's designs were based on integrating various structures with the natural terrain, his first priority being the transformation and enrichment of the landscape itself.

In his later commissions, Ritchie's regard for natural settings has been less pronounced, as he has begun to refocus his attention on defining the architectural object itself. However, his interest in the critical relationship between technology and ecology is far from being abandoned. Rather, it has found new applications through experimentation with techniques and materials that are ecologically friendly and economically sound.

The open-air concert platform for Paxton's landscape bowl at Crystal Palace Park in south London is a sculptural structure lying next to a small lake, in the center of a clearing that has been made into a natural amphitheater. Its power and plasticity derive from the abstract form created by two intersecting planes, and the rough, burnished red of Corten steel, reminiscent of the metallic sculptures of Richard Serra.

Although never executed, Ritchie's recent design for the Tower Bridge Theatre in London, which was intended as a temporary replacement for Covent Garden while the latter was being restored, was once again based on walls in natural stone supported by stainless steel mesh. In Terrasson, as well as at the Royal Albert Dock Rowing Club and Boathouse, the same technique was employed to emphasize the contrast between a heavy, solid foundation and a light, transpar-

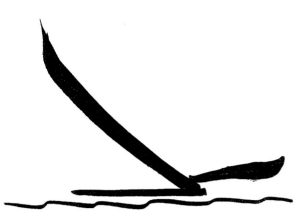

Open-air concert platform, Crystal Palace Park,
London

ent superstructure, where crude, primitive materials were meant to highlight the airy elegance and technical refinement of the glass surfaces. In the Tower Bridge Theatre project, the gabion wall served neither as a pseudo-naturalistic foundation (Terrasson), nor as a ready-made fiction (the nautical club on the Thames). Here, it lost the undifferentiated compactness of a retaining wall and became instead the wall of an actual building.

A layer of finer-grained stone marked the foundation, while the framework of folded steel plates supporting the gabion walls displayed a regular, quilted pattern formed by indentations between each section that allowed the stone fill to expand with the softness of a fabric. Within the framework mesh, however, there was a simple metallic grid that prevented the possible spray of pebbles, highlighting the contrast between geometric precision and common, ordinary materials that reminds one of Richard Long's "Circles."

The overall effect was one of alienation and even brutality: The texture of the gabion walls was reminiscent of the retaining walls normally used by road and railway construction crews to guard against rockfall, and as such, evoked very different images of distance and visibility. Recessed areas, windows, and supporting poles for flags and banners also had unusual forms and dimensions, further reinforcing the enigmatic quality of the walls. Here, Ritchie intended to go beyond the concept of lightness and transparency as the ultimate design objective: The technical refinement of the glass paneling in the front foyer, as opposed to the primitive allusions contained in the walls, only served to heighten the hybrid, ambiguous quality of the building.

Ritchie's architectural statement was also radical in the sense that it carried his goal of achieving maximum results at minimum cost ("more from less") to the ultimate extreme. This was made possible by the sheer inventiveness of his complex design, which used manual labor, and a highly original mix of industrial and natural materials and sophisticated technologies and simple techniques. Ritchie's need to explore new directions is currently shared by only a few of his contemporaries. However, as we contemplate the power and drama of the proposed designs for the stone walls of Tower Bridge Theatre, we can only hope that through the harnessing and intelligent use of the potentialities of high technology, it will be possible to open a new debate on the objectives and techniques of tomorrow's architecture and its leading proponents.

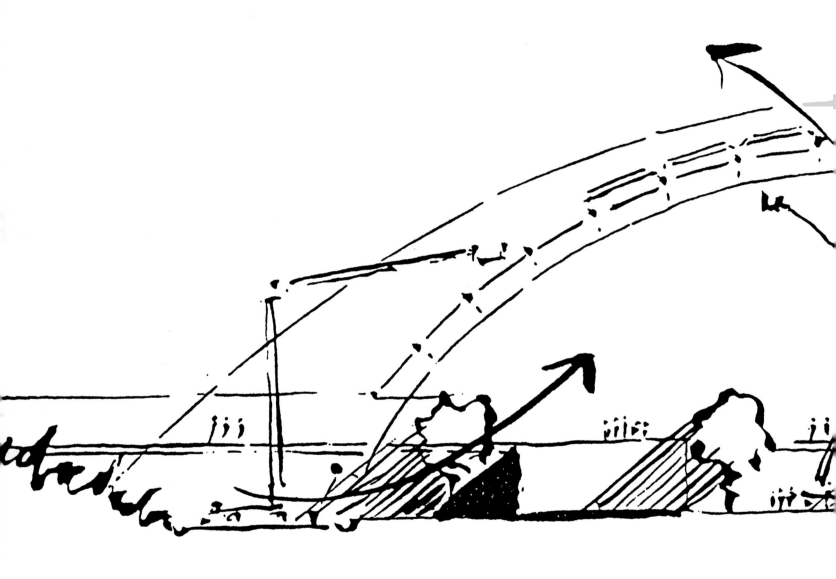

klima w

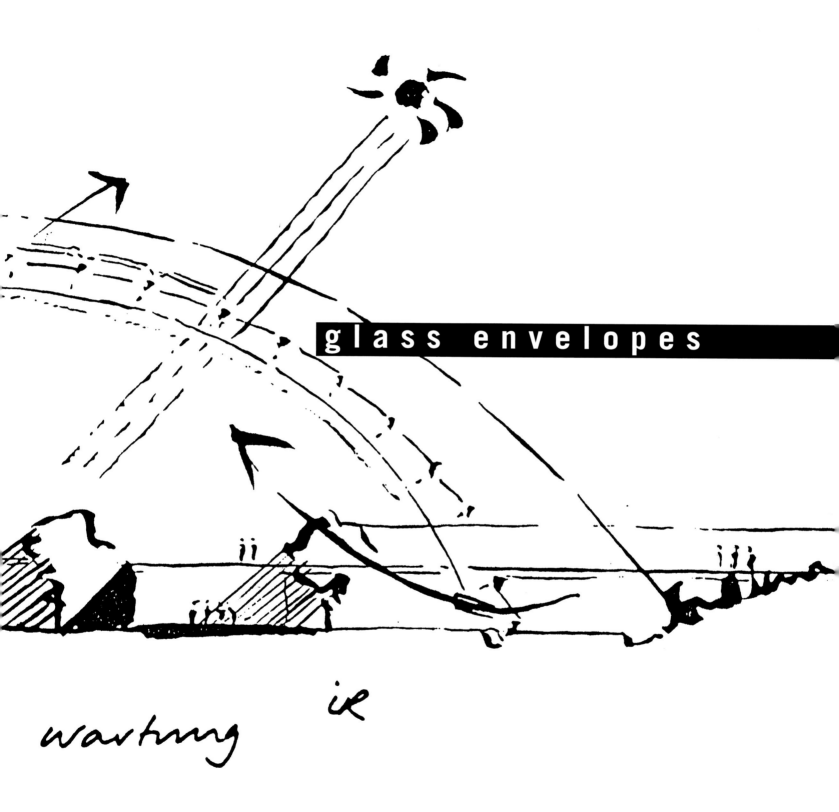

**glass envelopes**

### SURFACES

THE CONCERN WE HAVE WITH SURFACES HAS TO DO
WITH THE BOUNDARY BETWEEN THE INSIDE AND OUT-
SIDE OF AN ENVIRONMENT, THEIR DIALOGUE,
WHETHER AT THE SPIRITUAL OR THE PHYSICAL LEVEL.
WE TRY TO HUNT OUT THE ENVIRONMENTAL PERFOR-
MANCE OF SKINS AT THE SAME TIME AS A SENSUALI-
TY OF RELATIONSHIP THAT HUMAN BEINGS WILL PER-
CEIVE AND FEEL
BETWEEN INSIDE
AND
OUTSIDE.

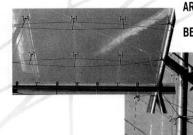

### HISTORY

THE HISTORY OF ARCHITECTURE HAS BEEN
THE STORY OF THE WAY IN WHICH LIGHT
ENTERS BUILDINGS: FIRST THROUGH SMALL OPEN-
INGS MADE IN SOLID WALLS AND ON THE ROOF, THEN
BY THE INTRODUCTION OF THE USE OF GLASS, WHICH
WAS STILL CUT INTO SMALL PIECES, AND TODAY, WITH
ENVELOPES MADE ENTIRELY OF GLASS. THE STORY OF
ARCHITECTURE'S DOMINION OVER THE RELATIONSHIP
BETWEEN GRAVITAS AND LEVITAS BEGINS TOWARDS
THE MIDDLE OF THE 19TH CENTURY,
AND IS BASED ON GLASS.

### GLASS

THIS UBIQUITOUS MATERIAL'S UNIQUENESS
LIES IN ITS ABILITY TO REFRACT AND REFLECT
LIGHT. IT IS PHENOMENAL. ITS DURABLE SURFACE
CAN TAKE A MULTITUDE OF TEXTURED SURFACE
TREATMENTS WHICH NO OTHER MATERIAL CAN
APPROACH—YET CONTINUE TO REFRACT LIGHT.

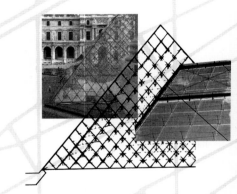

## TRANSPARENCY

GLASS CAN BE GRADUATED FROM TRANSPARENCY THROUGH DEGREES OF TRANSLUCENCY TO OPACITY; MACRO AND MICRO ETCHED WITH MACHINE, SAND AND ACID ETCHED, PATTERN AND PROFILE ROLLED, BODY COLOURED, STAINED, ENAMELLED, PAINTED, FIRED, AND PRINTED.

## ENVELOPES

TRANSPARENT ENVELOPES ACCEPT NATURAL LIGHT AS IT IS, WITH ITS CONTINUOUSLY CHANGING QUALITIES, MODIFYING IT SPECTRALLY AS IT PASSES THROUGH GLASS. TRANSPARENCY IS RARELY AN ARCHITECTURAL COMPOSITION OF LIGHT BUT A DYNAMIC SATURATION OF SPACE, A SITUATION WHICH NEARLY ALWAYS REQUIRES THE CONTROL (AND SOMETIMES THE QUALITY) OF SUNLIGHT BY SHADING. SHADING DESIGN CAN CONSEQUENTLY CREATE A STRONG EXTERNAL OR INTERNAL ARCHITECTURAL COMPOSITION. TRANSPARENCY IS SIMULTANEOUSLY THE NEGATION OF LIGHT AND ITS TOTALITY.

## PERFORMANCE

WHILE OUR DESIGNS HAVE OFTEN EXPLORED THE STRUCTURAL AND ENERGY PERFORMANCE OF CERTAIN MATERIALS TO HELP CREATE SPATIAL ENVIRONMENTS, ONE OF OUR CURRENT CONCERNS, AS ILLUSTRATED BY THE EXPERIMENTAL CULTURAL GREENHOUSE IN TERRASSON, AND OUR DESIGN APPROACH FOR A NEW OPERA HOUSE AT TOWER BRIDGE, IS TO CREATE A LESS EXPENSIVE ARCHITECTURE USING MATERIAL WHICH IS LESS AND LESS PROCESSED BY INDUSTRY, WHILE MAINTAINING THE PLEASURE OF LIGHT AND SPACE IN ARCHITECTURE.

*IAN RITCHIE*

## Experimental Greenhouse, Terrasson-Lavilledieu

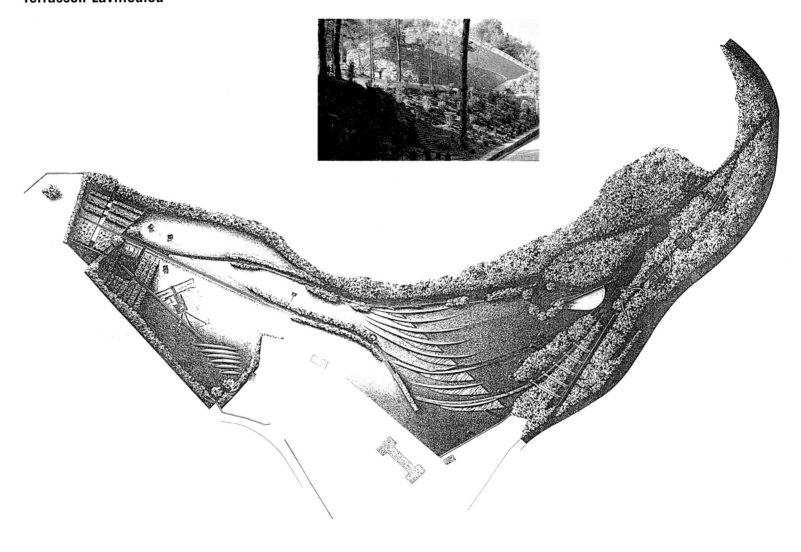

The Terrasson greenhouse, which has been carved out of the topography of the park, may be observed from three different perspectives: a tangential view of the roof, where the horizontal glass surface reflects portions of the park, the surrounding landscape, and the town; below, where the massive wall of rock seems to be an extension of the hilltop; and inside, where the space is defined by the juxtaposition of the gabion wall and the glass roof.

The quality of light in the interior, which changes constantly throughout the day, highlights the relationship between the two dominant materials—stone and glass—and their natural setting.

The project is based on the idea of a unified space, illuminated by a roof built entirely of glass. The objective is to create both a quiet, peaceful, internal environment, shielded from any view of the park, and an external environment, where the reflections of the roof lead the eye toward the treetops and the sky.

From the main entranceway, facing west, the visitor travels over a walkway raised two meters above the ground, and then descends the steps leading to the amphitheater, a place for rest and relaxation

that is used primarily for public performances. To the north, the curved wall, which is formed by blocks of stone contained in a stainless steel mesh, is surmounted by a row of lemon trees. Due to the transparency of the roof, it also receives the southern rays of the sun.

Along the south edge is the gallery, measuring approximately four and a half meters long and three meters high, which houses a research center, a bookstore, a coffee shop with an outdoor terrace, and public facilities. Equipped with computers, video projectors, slides, and films, this space is intended for seminars, lectures, and exhibitions.

The south side of the greenhouse has been left exposed to the open air in order to avoid an excess of humidity. Eventually, it may be protected by a glass screen, depending upon the way in which the internal microenvironment reacts to different situations.

Opposite page, top: Detail of the wall. Opposite page, center: Site plan. Above: Elevated view of the greenhouse, showing the glass surface of the roof.

Right: Perspective of the interior; partial view of the glass roof. Bottom: Longitudinal section through the amphitheater, facing north.

Opposite page, top: Partial views of the entranceway and amphitheater. Bottom: Longitudinal section through the amphitheater, facing south.

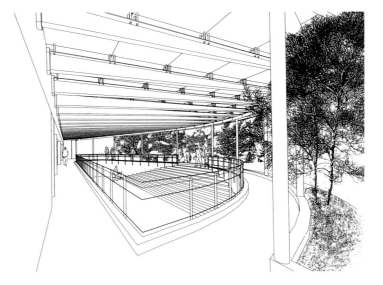 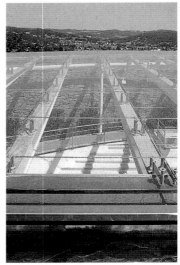

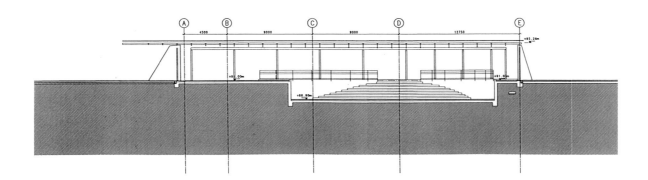

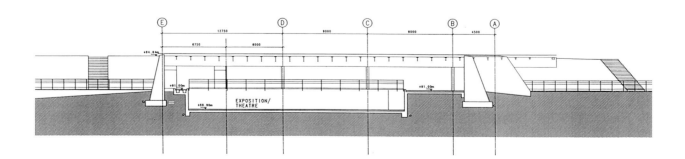

Left: Transverse section of the amphitheater.
Right: Partial view of the stone wall. Bottom:
Roof elevation.

Opposite page, top: View of the west entranceway, which leads to the walkway around the
amphitheater. Bottom: Greenhouse elevation.
Surrounded by the raised walkway, the space is
divided between the amphitheater, which is
exposed to constant shifts in the quality of natural light, and the more sheltered internal environment of the research center.

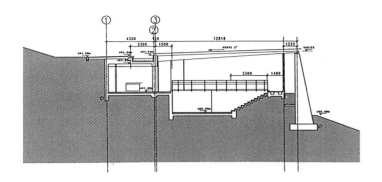

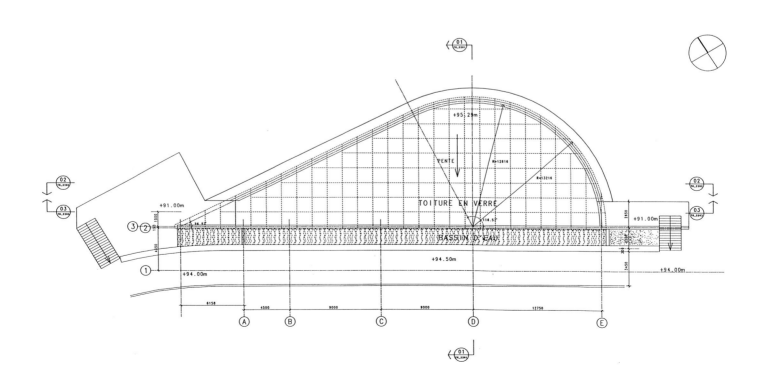

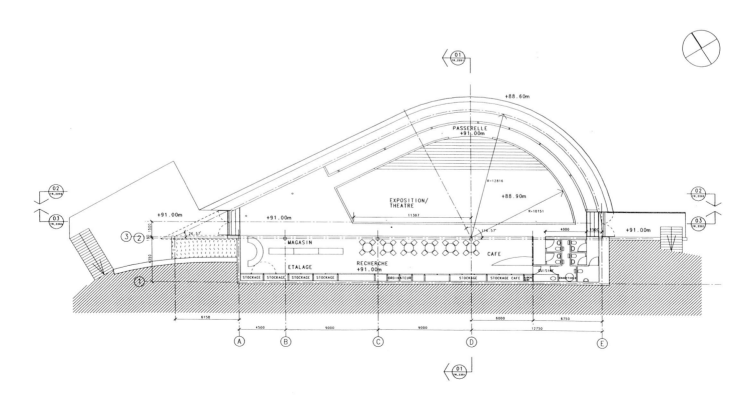

## TERRASSON - "SERRE"

### CONCEPTS ENVIRONNEMENTAUX

L'enveloppe du bâtiment fournira une protection adéquate contre les éléments vent, eau, et ciel.

L'environnement interne est conçu comme l'équivalent d'un espace couvert protégé et coupé du vent. Il sera chaud en été et frais en hiver; cependant, les conditions internes devraient être plus favorables que les conditions externes.

### Conditions hivernales

L'ouverture se situant autour du bord du toit permettra une ventilation adéquate pour empêcher une montée d'humidité. Ceci limitera le risque de condensation sur le toit en verre.

Pendant la journée, le soleil hivernal aidera à réchauffer l'espace jusqu'à 8° C au-dessus des conditions extérieures.

Le mur intérieur orienté au sud agira comme un collecteur solaire. Sa masse fournira une stabilité thermique.

Certains espaces internes tels que café, magasin, peuvent requérir un chauffage pour maintenir des conditions de confort. Le chauffage le plus efficace sera réalisé par une séparation thermique de l'aire du balcon, par exemple, par un écran "isolant".

### Résumé

L'environnement interne sera frais car le bâtiment ne pourra pas retenir la chaleur.

Les températures seront modérées par les matériaux du bâtiment représentant une masse exposée importante . Le gain solaire augmentera considérablememt la température interne pendant la journée.

Le bâtiment sera bien ventilé ce qui éliminera l'humidité créée, et, par conséquent, réduira le risque de condensation sur le toit en verre.

As the building is designed not to retain heat, the internal environment is always comfortable. The temperature is moderated by the massive nature of the construction materials, as well as variations in the amount of sunlight received during the day. The structure is also well-ventilated to prevent the accumulation of humidity, thereby avoiding condensation on the glass roof.

## Conditions estivales

Le toit vitré permettra une pénétration maximale de lumière et d'énergie.

Un pare-soleil sera nécessaire afin de protéger à haut niveau les occupants d'un accroissement solaire direct et d'une augmentation de chaleur rayonnante causée par des surfaces vitrées et empêchera le chauffage du sol et des surfaces internes.

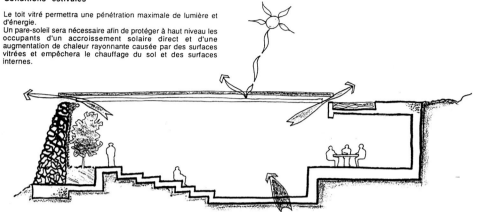

L'eau vaporisée sur le mur aidera à rafraîchir le mur et, par conséquent, contribue au confort par une radiation froide.

La masse importante du mur exposée fournira une stabilité thermique.

La forme, la hauteur et la construction du bâtiment génèrent une ventilation naturelle grâce au loi naturelle de l'air chaud qui monte, et à des ouvertures placées afin de maximiser cette ventilation.

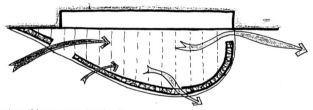

Les mouvements des vents extérieurs augmenteront cette ventilation à travers l'espace.

## Résumé

Les températures extérieures seront élevées dû à un élément solaire puissant.

L'environnement interne sera contrôlé par des moyens passifs pour fournir des conditions thermiques satisfaisantes. La température de l'air sera semblable aux températures extérieures; un pare-soleil devra être fourni pour protéger les occupants des radiations directes de soleil.

Un pare-soleil à haut niveau empêchera le bâtiment de surchauffer.

La ventilation se fera naturellement à travers l'ouverture se trouvant au bord du toit et par les portes d'entrée.

Le mur au nord, de part sa masse, sert à "amortir" la température interne et lorsque ce mur est arrosé avec de l'eau, un effet de fraîcheur rayonnant se fera sentir.

When the external temperature is elevated, the internal microclimate is controlled by passive systems that maintain a high-quality environment, including a solar deflector located above the greenhouse, which also protects visitors from the direct rays of the sun.

Natural ventilation is made possible through the opening situated along the edge of the roof. The massive stone wall to the north serves to absorb the effects of sudden rises in temperature and, when dampened, to cool down the interior.

Opposite page: Detail of the gabion stone wall and stainless steel mesh, surmounted by the edge of the glass roof. The opening between the two structures provides for natural ventilation of the interior.

Above: Partial view of the amphitheater, showing the elevated walkway and glass roof. A row of lemon trees separates the wall from the walkway.

# Reina Sofia Museum of Modern Art, Madrid

The initial idea for this project, which came from the Spanish Minister of Culture, was inspired by his visit to La Villette Park in Paris, where the RFR studio had designed the Ecology Gallery for the Museum of Science and Technology. Ritchie's three circulation towers for the new Reina Sofia Museum of Modern Art in Madrid, consisting of thin 12-story-high steel fins enclosing glass elevators that support a tension-braced tubular steel frame at roof level, were part of the transformation of the city's main hospital building, constructed in the 18th century by Francisco Sabatini. The renovation took place in three stages, including a complete restoration of the facilities under the supervision of Antonio Fernandez Alba, followed by a restructuring of the basement and ground floor to accommodate a coffee house and restaurant designed by André Richard, an auditorium by Bach and Mora, and public facilities by Torres and Lapeña. At this point, in 1986, the building was opened to the public. The third and final stage, Antonio Vasquez de Castro and José Luis Iñiquez de Onzoño's design for a new National Center for the Arts, was completed in 1990. The museum's inaugural ceremony was highlighted by the presence of King Juan Carlos and Queen Sofia, who presided over the installation of Picasso's *Guernica*.

Clockwise from top right: Detail of the structural support system for the glass panels; perspective with partial view of the towers; view of the main facade.

The design and construction of the towers were based on four main principles:
Minimalism: Economy of materials and simplicity of form.
Modernity: A visual expression of current, and future, attitudes toward design and technology.
Performance: Facilitating the circulation of thousands of daily visitors; achieving a degree of transparency that softens the visual impact with the exterior while allowing for complete visibility of the interior, as individuals wait on line, and, in a more spectacular way, as they go up in the elevators; finally, during their tour of the museum, providing an opportunity for people to once again make contact with the outside world as they pass through the transparent towers.

Design: Complete separation of the external structure, which bears the vertical weight of the glass walls, and the internal structure, which is designed to resist the horizontal stress of wind load. The entire skin of glass is suspended from the stainless steel plate of the roof. Each panel of glass is supported individually, so that the differential between the thermal movement of the glass and stainless steel is entirely absorbed by the coil-spring tension cables situated between the panels.

# Main Hall, International Exhibition Center, Leipzig

Exploring the potentialities of transparency, which was the primary objective of the Leipzig project, led to the concept of a single-layer, grid shell in the form of a barrel vault that supports the internal transparent envelope. The ultimate impression of transparency is enhanced by the use of low-iron "white" glass, as well as the shape of the vault itself, which was designed so that the view out of the hall in all directions is perpendicular to the surface of the glass, thereby limiting perceived reflections.

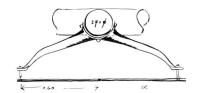

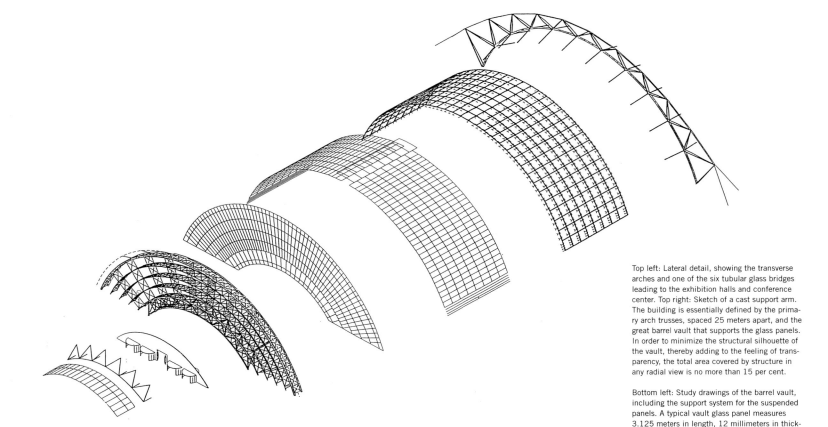

Top left: Lateral detail, showing the transverse arches and one of the six tubular glass bridges leading to the exhibition halls and conference center. Top right: Sketch of a cast support arm. The building is essentially defined by the primary arch trusses, spaced 25 meters apart, and the great barrel vault that supports the glass panels. In order to minimize the structural silhouette of the vault, thereby adding to the feeling of transparency, the total area covered by structure in any radial view is no more than 15 per cent.

Bottom left: Study drawings of the barrel vault, including the support system for the suspended panels. A typical vault glass panel measures 3.125 meters in length, 12 millimeters in thickness, and weighs 190 kilograms.

The hall's simple two-level hierarchy consists of primary arch trusses spaced 25 meters apart along the entire length of the gallery, and a secondary grid shell divided into square modules and completely devoid of framing and diagonal cross-bracing. The steel structure of primary trusses and grid shell is hot-dipped galvanized and finished with silver-gray paint. There is no structural connection between the grid shell and the endwalls, so that wind loads on them are not attracted to the end bays of the grid shell. Consequently, grid-shell members are not locally changed, and the visual sim-

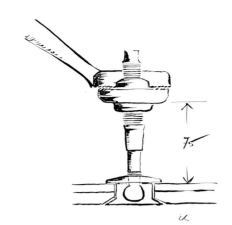

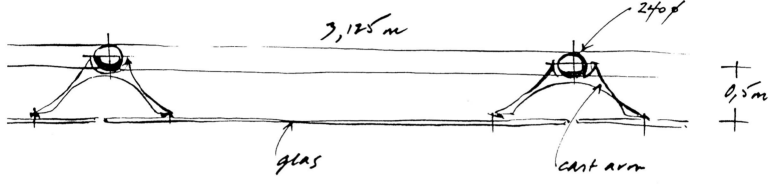

The hall measures 244 meters in length by 80 meters in width. The overall height is 35 meters. The total weight of the steel structure is 2,070 tons. The construction period (structure and glass) consisted of 10 months, seven of which involved the installation of the glass panels.

The transverse arches that stabilize the entire structure, which are tapered toward the center, are visibly separate from the shell. The upper arch spans across the service roads, anchoring the gallery solidly to the ground.

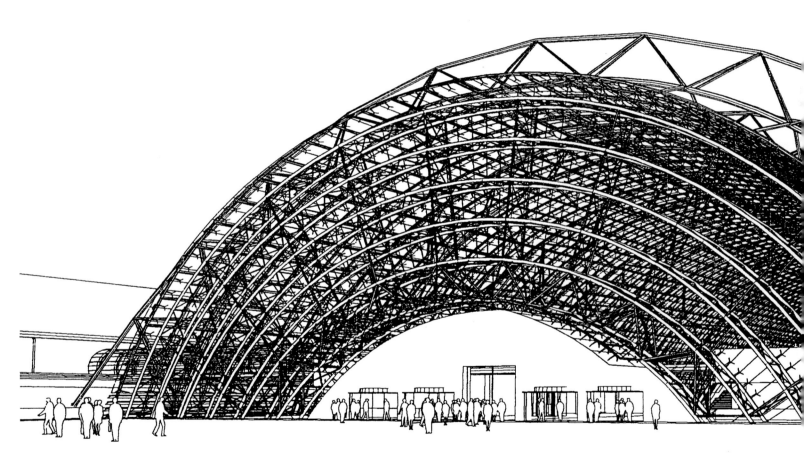

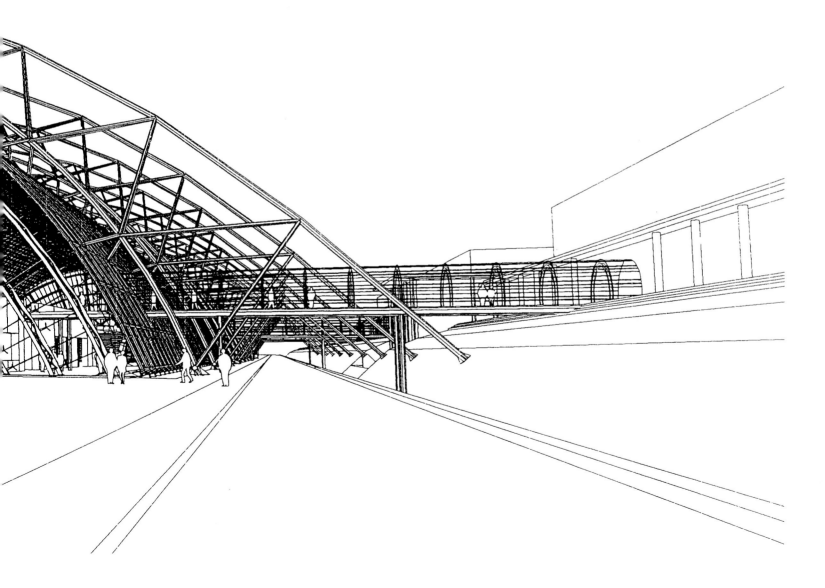

**pavilions**

## INDUSTRY

TODAY IN THE CONSTRUCTION INDUSTRY,AFTER DECADES DOMINATED BY THE POWER OF INDUSTRIAL PRODUCTION OF MONOTONOUS PROJECTS RESULTING FROM MANAGEMENT AND MANUFACTURING METHODS SEEKING EVER MORE ECONOMIES, THERE IS NOW A NEED TO INJECT ART INTO INDUSTRY. THE DESIGN, ENGINEERING AND MANUFACTURE OF PRIMARY MATERIALS INTO PRODUCTS WHICH CARRY THE SIGNATURE OF THE DESIGNER, THE PRESENCE OF THE HUMAN HAND, MIND AND HEART HAS BECOME ESSENTIAL IN ORDER THAT INDUSTRY NOT ONLY SERVES MAN'S MATERIAL NEEDS, BUT ALSO HIS SENSIBILITIES.

## MATERIALS

SOME OF OUR WORK HAS AND WILL CONTINUE TO BE CONTROVERSIAL IN THE SENSE OF MAKING INDUSTRY RETHINK ITS ATTITUDE, CHALLENGING ITS DOMINANCE WHILE AT THE SAME TIME ATTEMPTING TO ACHIEVE THOSE HUMAN QUALITIES IN MATERIAL PRODUCTS THROUGH THEIR SCALE, POSITION AND CONTRIBUTION TO THE OVERALL ARCHITECTURE. IN ORDER TO COMMUNICATE THIS TO THE INDUSTRIES WITH WHOM WE WORK, IT IS NECESSARY TO ACQUIRE A DEEP UNDERSTANDING OF THE TRUE NATURE OF MATERIALS,TO LEARN HOW TO MANIPULATE THESE MATERIALS IN AN AESTHETIC MANNER AND TO APPRECIATE HOW INDUSTRY CAN PRODUCE THE PRODUCTS FROM THEM.

## TRANSFER

THIS APPROACH IS NOT THAT OF TAKING INDUSTRIAL PRODUCTS FROM OTHER INDUSTRIES (MARINE, AEROSPACE) AND EXECUTING AN AESTHETIC TECHNOLOGICAL TRANSFER, OR TAKING SOCIETY'S INDUSTRIAL WASTE TO PRODUCE ON-OFF ARCHITECTURAL ART PIECES, BUT IS AN APPROACH WHICH SEEKS TO INFECT INDUSTRY IN ITS OWN HOME WITH THESE HUMAN AND SENSIBLE VALUES. WE BELIEVE THAT IT IS HERE THAT CHANGE IS NECESSARY WHICH WILL ALLOW NEW ARCHITECTURES TO EMERGE. THIS APPROACH RECOGNISES THE ROLE OF INDUSTRY IN OUR SOCIETY, UTILISES THE CREATIVE AND ECONOMIC POTENTIAL OF COMPUTERS AND COMPUTER-CONTROLLED MACHINES TO PROVIDE THE NECESSARY PRODUCTS TO SERVE SOCIETY'S NEEDS THROUGH TAILOR-MADE VOLUME PRODUCTION, AND NOT JUST FOR THE PRIVATE AND PRIVILEGED INDULGENCE OF A FEW.

## SOCIETY

AN ARCHITECTURE WHICH USES MATERIALS TO REFLECT THE CONDITION OF SOCIETY, WHERE THESE MATERIALS ARE USED IN THEIR PRIMARY STATE RATHER THAN AS PRODUCTS, E.G. METAL SHEET COIL, AND ENGAGES CRAFTSMEN TO MANIPULATE THEM, WITH OR WITHOUT THE USE OF COMPUTERS, IN THE FACTORY OR IN THEIR SITE ASSEMBLY, CAN REPRESENT A 20TH-CENTURY EVOLUTION OF THE ARTS AND CRAFTS TRADITION.

## DEVELOPMENT

THROUGH THE DEVELOPMENT OF NEW TECHNOLOGIES, OUR OWN ARCHITECTURE WILL BECOME MORE DYNAMIC AND LESS MATERIAL, IN THE SENSE THAT TRANSPARENT STRUCTURAL MATERIALS SUCH AS GLASS AND DIAMOND FILMS WILL BECOME THE SUPPORT MEDIUM FOR HOLOGRAMS, MINIATURISED LASERS AND BIOGENETIC COATINGS OFFERING THE POSSIBILITIES TO IMPROVE ENERGY EFFICIENCY, TO CREATE INTERACTIVE BUILDING SURFACES TO BOTH USER AND THE ENVIRONMENT AND RELEASE NEW CREATIVE ENERGIES IN THE DESIGN AND VISUAL PLEASURE OF OUR BUILDINGS.

## DIALOGUE

OUR PRECONCEPT, WHICH IS NOT THE IDEA OF A BUILDING, BUT THE IDEA OF WHAT WE WISH TO EXPRESS (ART), IS A DIALOGUE BETWEEN PERMANENCE AND FRAGILITY. YOU MIGHT SAY THAT THE EARTH IS THE FRAGILE BIT, BUT I WOULD SUGGEST THAT IS ONLY THE SURFACE IDEA IN OUR MINDS TODAY. WHAT WE ARE REALLY SAYING IS THE EARTH IS 'PERMANENT' AND THAT'S THE WAY IT WILL BE (WITH OR WITHOUT US). I WOULD PUT FORWARD THE PRECONCEPT THAT THE EARTH IS PERMANENT, WHILE THE INFORMATION AGE IS FRAGILE AND EPHEMERAL. THIS IS ALSO AMBIGUOUS IN THAT WE ARE PROBABLY SUGGESTING THAT IT IS WE HUMANS WHO ARE EPHEMERAL.

*IAN RITCHIE*

# B8 Building, Stockley Park, Heathrow

Completed in the space of only 36 weeks, the B8 office/research facility at Stockley Park industrial complex, located near Heathrow Airport, comprises more than 9,000 square meters of work space spread out over three floors. On each floor, inside a modular grid measuring 9 x 9 meters, there are two entirely separate 18 x 63 meter surfaces that surround a central atrium. The building envelope is constructed of the same double-pane Pilkington glass that was employed for the towers of the Reina Sofia Museum. The reinforced transparent panels, which are partially opaqued by a white ceramic patina, are attached by four clamps to a steel structure supported by suspension rods made of extruded aluminum.

The structural skin is composed of a 12-millimeter-thick outer glass sheet, a 16-millimeter air space, and a 6-millimeter inner glass sheet. The only variation is found in the skylights, where the outer sheet is 15 millimeters thick. Large curved plates of perforated stainless steel, which are utilized as solar deflectors, are situated on the east, south, and west facades, while the central atrium is covered by a skylight that provides an abundance of natural illumination to the innermost areas of the building.

Opposite page, top: Detail of the southwest
corner, with opaque glass panels and solar
deflectors. Opposite page, bottom: Site plan.

Above: View from the south, and right: plan of
the ground floor, both of which show the solar
deflectors on the east, south, and west facades.

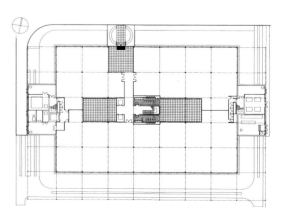

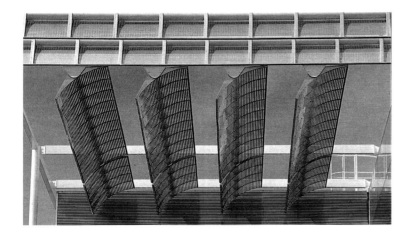

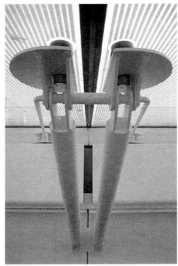

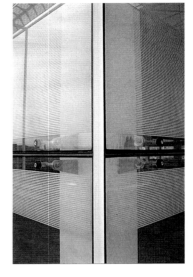

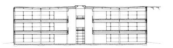

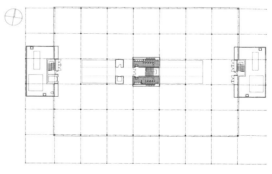

Top left: Partial view of the stainless steel solar deflectors. Top center: Partial view of the glass panel connection in the foyer. Top right: Partial view of a typical corner. Center: Transverse section of the central atrium. Bottom: Plan of a typical floor.

Opposite page: Detail of a corner; the glass panel, which has no cornice, is terminated by the stainless steel structure of the solar deflectors.

# Jubilee Line Extension, Bermondsey Station, London

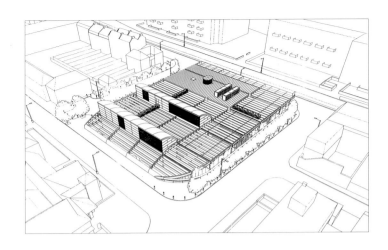

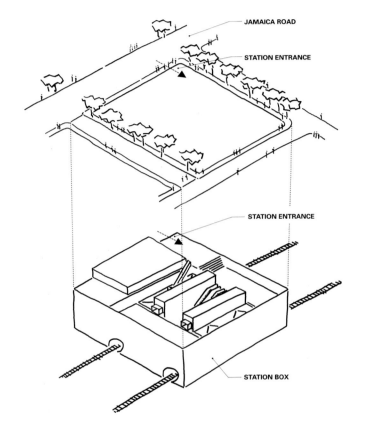

JAMAICA ROAD

STATION ENTRANCE

STATION ENTRANCE

STATION BOX

The Bermondsey Station project was based on two principal objectives: the maximum utilization of natural light, and the creation of a clear, immediately comprehensible space. At ground level, the station curves gently toward Jamaica Road, visually merging the external environment with the underlying structure. The roof is a transparent glass surface supported by a system of perforated steel beams to allow greater penetration of light. At certain hours of the day, the rays of the sun actually illuminate the train platforms. Night lighting was added in order to upgrade the immediate urban environment, as well as to permit ample visibility of the inner spaces.

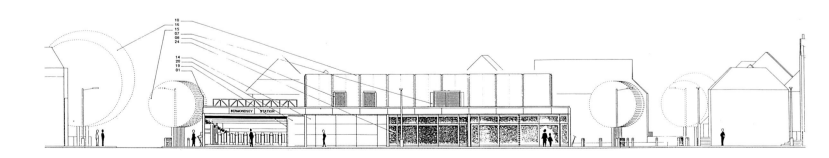

Opposite page, top: Aerial perspective view. Left: Axonometric drawing. Bottom: Jamaica Road elevation, with the main entranceway.

This page: Two views of the Bermondsey Station model. The transparency of the glass walls provides the maximum amount of natural lighting during the day; at night, it upgrades the quality of the immediate urban environment, and improves security.

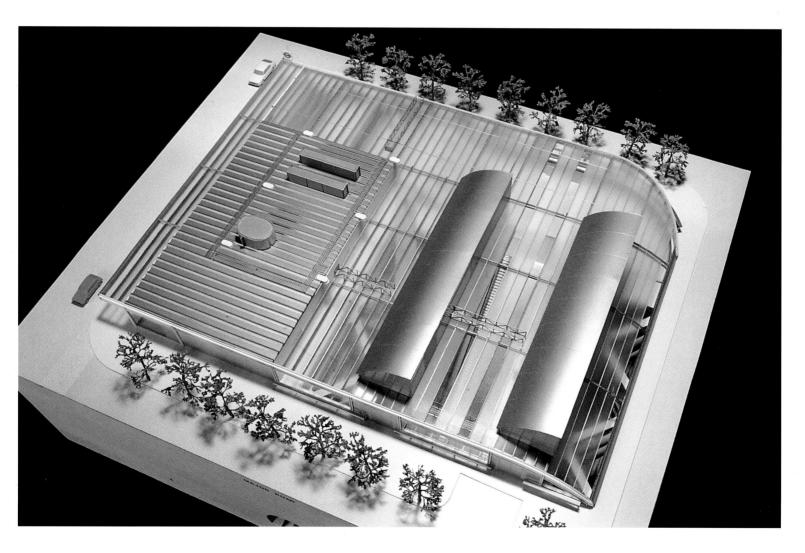

# Royal Albert Dock Rowing Club and Boathouse, London

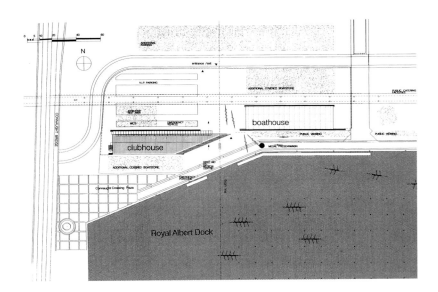

Left: Site plan. Bottom: Diagram showing the location of the rowing club and boathouse on the Thames River, in the area known as the London Docklands.

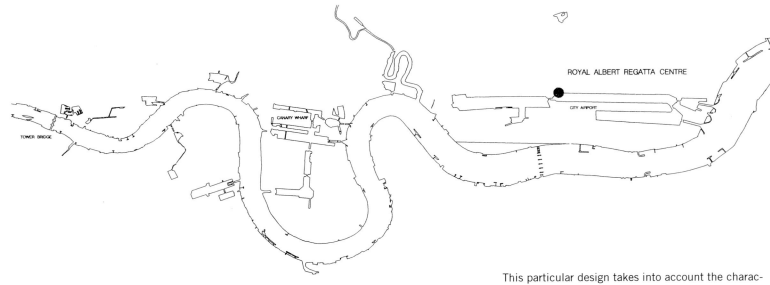

This particular design takes into account the characteristics of the immediate surroundings of London's Docklands, including the Thames River, equipment and infrastructures left over from the former port, and the new City Airport, which form a combined setting that calls for a strong architectural statement.
Due to the long, narrow space that was made available for the project, the rowing club and boathouse were

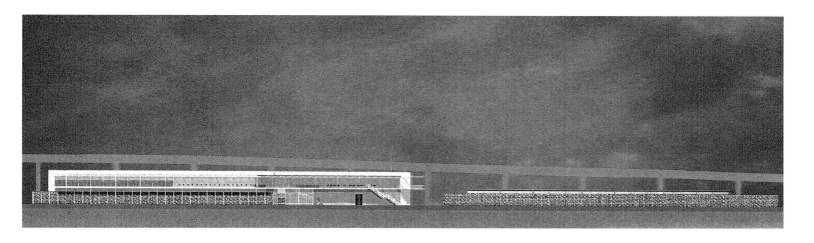

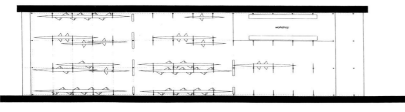

BOATHOUSE PLAN

Top: Thames River elevation with the club house on the left and the boathouse on the right.
Left: Detailed plan of the boathouse.
Bottom: Axonometric drawing of the boathouse. The basic configuration of the boathouse involves two long, parallel stone walls, and two shorter walls composed of metallic grid panels. Given the limited amount of available space, the overall structure is tightly contained. The boat slips, which have been designed for easy maneuverability and immediate accessibility, all have their own maintenance equipment. The facility also includes a boatyard for major repairs. The roof consists of a stainless steel plate forming three catenary arches between one beam and the next.

planned as separate buildings. The two facilities are situated along parallel gabion stone walls contained in a metallic grid. This low-cost technical solution, which has already been used for the greenhouse at Terrasson and the proposed Tower Bridge Theatre, assures both high thermal insulation and sufficient stability for lightweight structures with large glass surfaces.

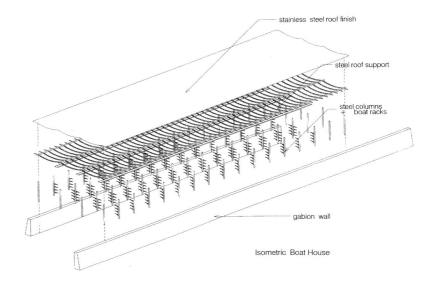

stainless steel roof finish

steel roof support

steel columns + boat racks

gabion wall

Isometric Boat House

49

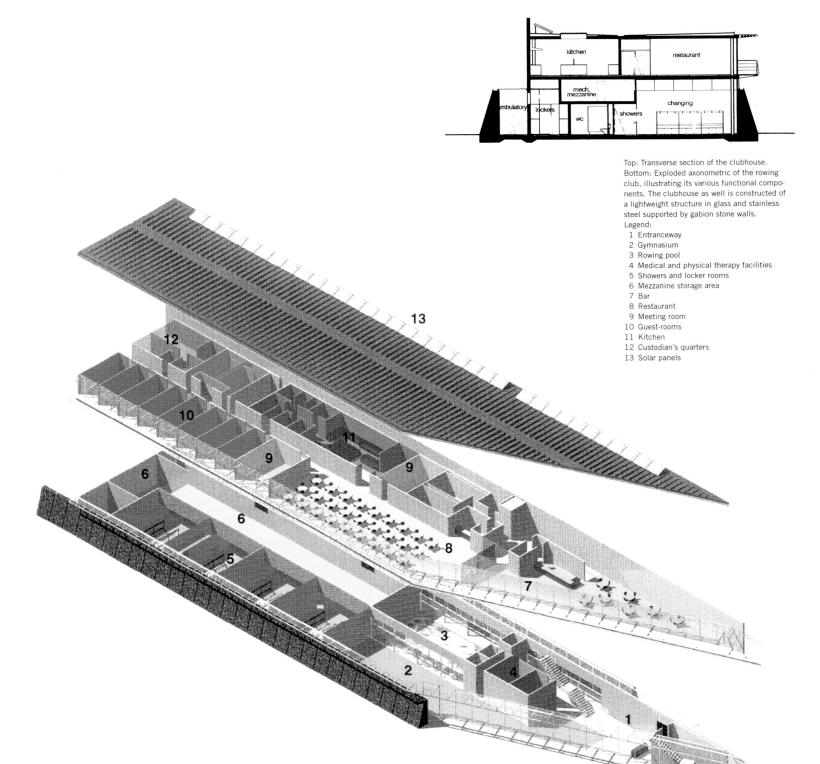

Top: Transverse section of the clubhouse.
Bottom: Exploded axonometric of the rowing club, illustrating its various functional components. The clubhouse as well is constructed of a lightweight structure in glass and stainless steel supported by gabion stone walls.
Legend:
 1 Entranceway
 2 Gymnasium
 3 Rowing pool
 4 Medical and physical therapy facilities
 5 Showers and locker rooms
 6 Mezzanine storage area
 7 Bar
 8 Restaurant
 9 Meeting room
10 Guest-rooms
11 Kitchen
12 Custodian's quarters
13 Solar panels

Top and bottom: Views of the clubhouse. The rowing club and boathouse are situated at Royal Albert Dock, an Olympic-sized harbor with a 2,000-meter-long racecourse. Located under the lee of a viaduct and close to the new City Airport, they are part of the city's overall plan to convert the former Docklands into housing units and various other facilities.

## Tower Bridge Theatre (Royal Opera House), London

The design for the Tower Bridge Theatre, which was never executed, was heavily influenced by the intended historical setting. Among the many distinct characteristics of the immediate environment were the sparkling waters of the Thames, the altered perception of space with the changing of the tides, the spectacular views and nighttime illumination of the Tower of London and Tower Bridge, the riverside park, and the embankments filled with tourists.

The theater's proposed structure was based primarily upon its function as an envelope for the auditorium. The main facade, which was to overlook the Thames, was a sheet of transparent, colorless glass, allowing magnificent views from multi-leveled foyers and a balcony under the overhang of the roof. In contrast, the other facades of the building, which were closed in, were composed of stainless steel mesh containing massive stone fill walls that recalled the tonalities of both the tower and its bridge. The two side walls, whose foundations were constructed of finer-grained stone, were crisscrossed by the grids containing the stone wall and highlighted by steel-framed punched windows. When viewed from the front, the building would seem to be made of stone; when viewed tangentially, its stainless steel mesh would create the illusion of a structure made of metal.

Opposite page, top: Photomontage of the south bank of the Thames, showing the proposed theater and Tower Bridge. Opposite page, bottom: Preliminary sketches.

Top: Ground floor plan showing immediate site surroundings, with existing parkland on the west side of the theater, and a new park planned for the east side. Center: Photomontage of the building at night. Bottom: Preliminary sketches. The main entrances and foyers were located on the north side, facing the park and the Thames.

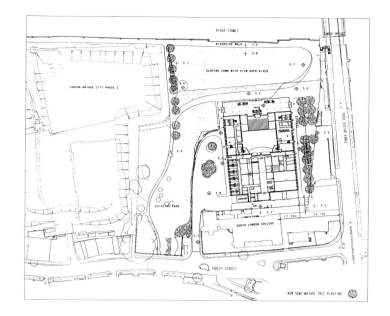

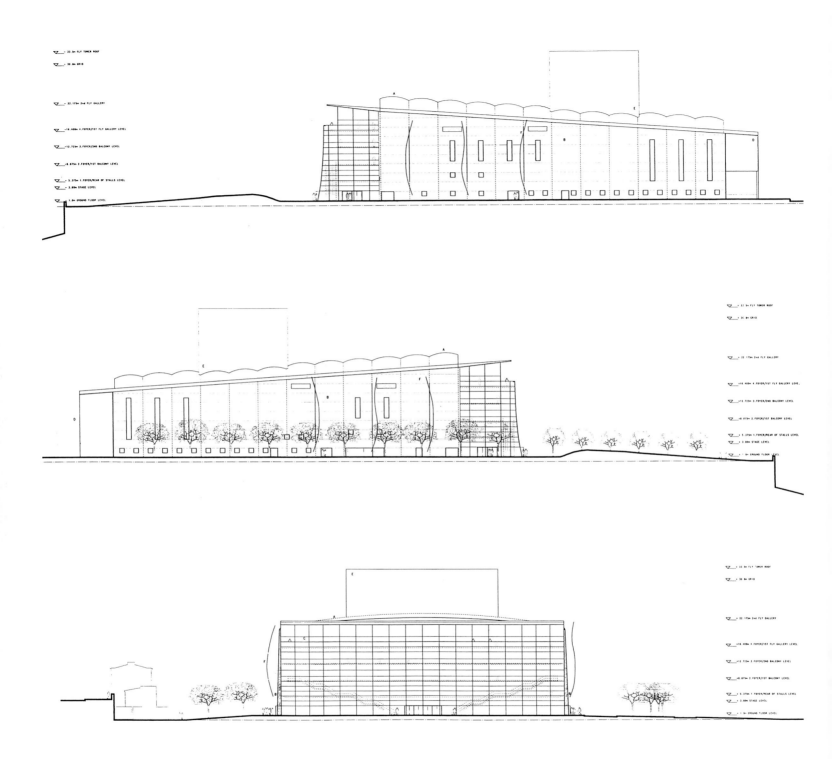

Top: West elevation. Center: East elevation. Bottom: View of the main facade (facing north), including the staircases that led from the foyers to the auditorium doors. The curvilinear elements located on the side walls indicate banners and flags.

Opposite page: View of the model as seen from the southwest. The south facade, whose wall was composed of hot-dipped galvanized corrugated metal panels, revealed the structural elements in the building's interior.

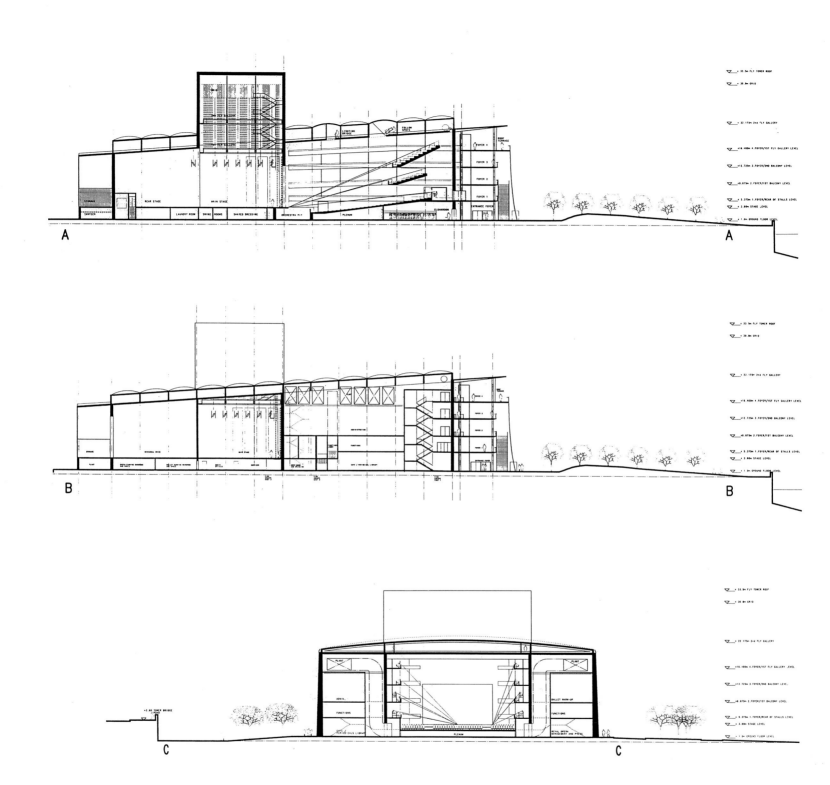

Opposite page: Top: Longitudinal section through loading dock, stage, fly tower, auditorium, and foyer. Center: Longitudinal section through lateral circulation space. Bottom: Transverse section through auditorium looking toward the stage.

Top: Computer generated interior perspective of stage and auditorium. Bottom: Plan view of auditorium with a capacity of 2,350 seats.

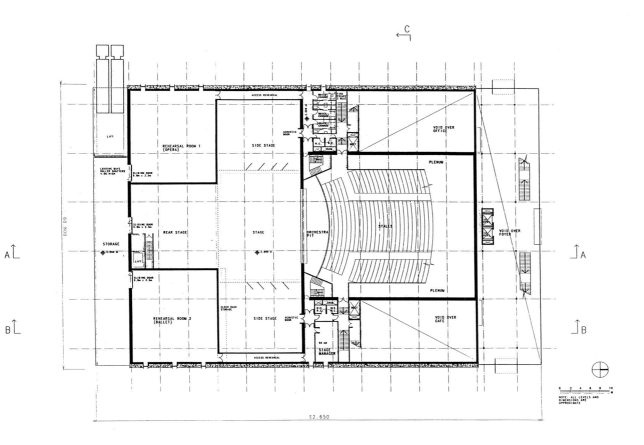

Opposite page: View of the model from the east.

Bottom left: Detail section of north wall. The completely transparent glass wall was planned to afford a full view of the exterior from all of the foyers. The balcony on the fourth level looked out on London Tower, Tower Bridge, and the Thames. Bottom right: Detail section of lateral walls, showing the inner metallic frame, steel columns, lightweight concrete fill, and stone wall contained by stainless steel mesh. The roof was composed of long-span arched steel trusses.

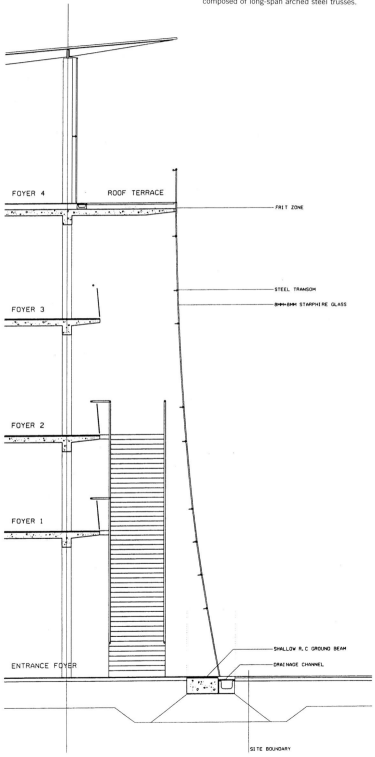

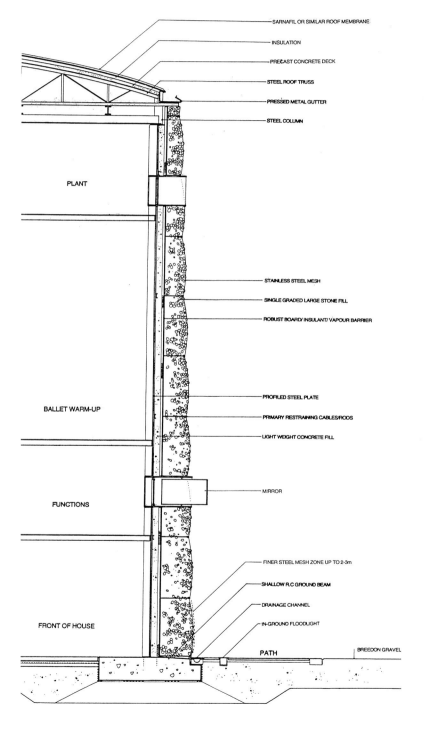

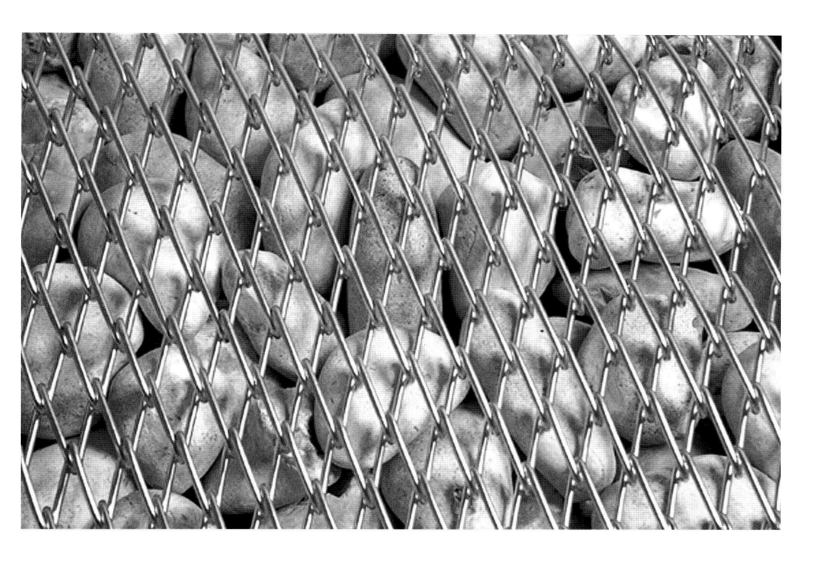

Opposite page: Detail of east elevation.
Above: Computer generated detail of exterior wall construction of the east and west elevations. The stainless steel mesh supported the metallic grid, which in turn contained the stone fill wall. The windows were recessed into the walls, with outer frames in folded stainless steel plate and inner frames in bronze.

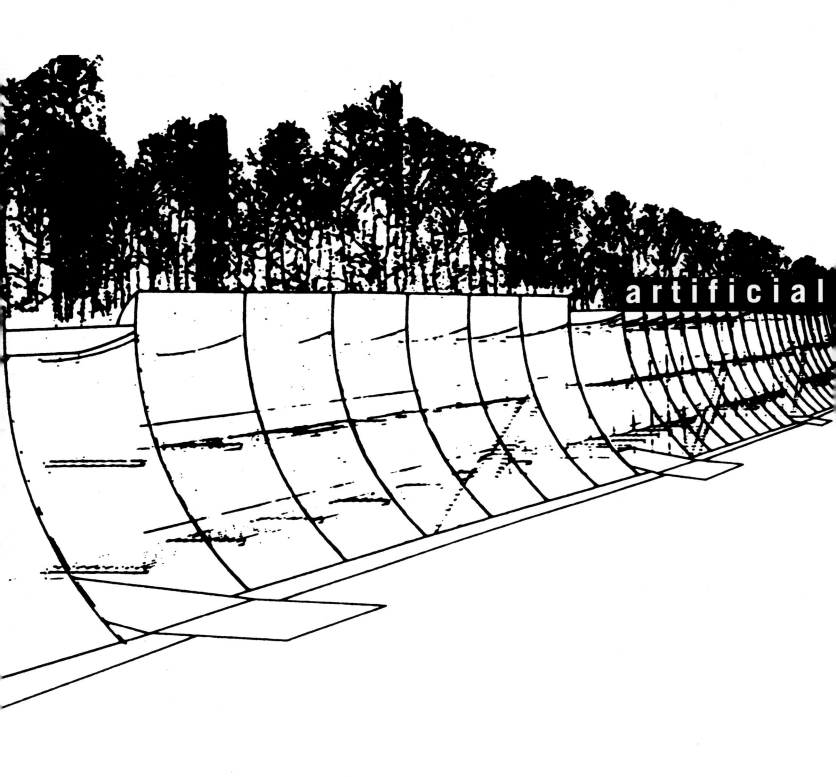

artificial

landscapes

### SCIENCE

APPRECIATION COMES FROM AWARENESS, SENSIBLE ACTION COMES FROM KNOWLEDGE, KNOWLEDGE COMES FROM SCIENCE AND RESEARCH, AND TECHNIQUE COMES FROM STRATEGIC POLICY MAKERS; POLICIES TO ENABLE CORRECT ACTION COME FROM GOVERNMENT. ONE FUNCTION OF SCIENCE IS TO HELP CONTROL THE WORLD WE LIVE IN; THE OTHER, WHICH IS MORE IMPORTANT, IS SIMPLY TO HELP US APPRECIATE IT.

### DESIGNERS

EACH GENERATION OF DESIGNERS MUST DETERMINE ITS OWN SOLUTIONS TO ARCHITECTURAL SPACE, BOTH EXTERNALLY AND INTERNALLY: SPACE WHICH IS IDEAL FOR THE PRESENTATION OF THE ART, SCIENCE, TECHNOLOGY AND ISSUES OF ITS OWN TIME. THIS IS IN THE SPIRIT OF MODERNITY, WHICH IS AT THE VERY CORE OF WESTERN CIVILISATION—RESEARCH WITHOUT PRECONCEIVED FORMULAE OR STYLISTIC PREJUDICES, AND THE CREATION OF THE MOST APPROPRIATE SOLUTIONS TO IMPROVE OUR UNDERSTANDING OF OURSELVES AND OUR ENVIRONMENT.

### ENVIRONMENT

THE FUNDAMENTAL PROBLEM FOR ME IS NEITHER STRUCTURAL NOR ARCHITECTURAL, BUT ENVIRON-MENTAL: TO FIND AN ENVIRONMENTALLY AESTHETIC RESPONSE OF SUCH QUALITY THAT IT WILL EXCITE AND SUSTAIN ALL THOSE INVOLVED IN THE COLLABORATION.

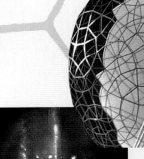

## VALUES

THE NEED TO MAKE EVIDENT HUMANITY AND INTELLIGENCE IN WHAT WE DESIGN SHOULD BE INDISPUTABLE. IT IS THIS WHICH DRIVES OUR DESIGN APPROACH. REAL PROGRESS FOR MANKIND AND A REAL SUSTAINABLE FUTURE FOR THE EARTH ARE BECOMING ESSENTIALLY THE SAME. ARCHITECTURAL AND ENGINEERING DESIGN AND CONSTRUCTION MUST DEAL WITH PROGRESS BY DRAWING UPON THE STRONG METAPHORICAL STEM OF THE HUMAN SPIRIT AND EARTHLY VALUES.

## GRAMMAR

THE GRAMMAR OF AESTHETICS IS COMPOSED NOT ONLY OF THE VISUAL, BUT ALSO OF THE POLITICAL, ECONOMIC AND MORAL LANGUAGES. HUMANITY AND INTELLIGENCE HAVE AS MUCH TO DO WITH THE PROCESS OF DECISION-MAKING AS THEY DO WITH THE TANGIBLE ARTIFACTS WHICH RESULT FROM OUR APPLICATION OF SCIENCE, TECHNOLOGY AND ECONOMICS. GOETHE DESCRIBED GOOD ARCHITECTURE AS FROZEN MUSIC, BUT IN REALITY IT IS ALSO FROZEN POLITICS, ECONOMICS AND POWER.

## INFORMATION

TODAY, THE EFFECTS OF TECHNICAL INNOVATION AND INDUSTRIAL ACTIVITY ON OUR ENVIRONMENT HAVE BECOME MUCH MORE TANGIBLE TO MANY MORE PEOPLE. THE BELIEF THAT WE CAN CONTROL THIS ACTIVITY IS STILL ESSENTIALLY AN OPTIMISTIC IDEA. THE CONTROLLING ASPECT CONCERNS THE NATURE OF GOVERNMENT. FREEDOM OF INFORMATION AND THE DISSEMINATION OF BETTER INFORMATION ON THE DAMAGE WE ARE DOING TO THE ENVIRONMENT WOULD CREATE A WIDER AWARENESS AND KNOWLEDGE, WHICH COULD ENABLE MORE PEOPLE TO ACT MORALLY AND INTELLIGENTLY WITHIN A WIDER CONTEXT (DEFINITION) OF SOCIETY AND GOVERNMENT.

If you are thinking
sow seed.
If you are thinking
plant a tree.
If you are thinking
educate the people

*IAN RITCHIE*

# Pearl of the Gulf, Dubai

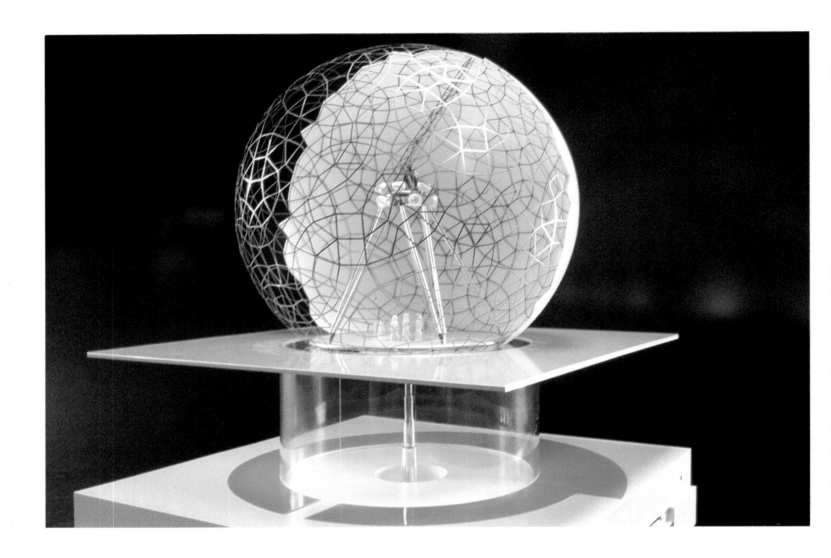

In an effort to improve the ecology of its coastline, the city of Dubai has created a parkland area along the edge of the Persian Gulf. Situated in this new linear landscape, the Pearl is a perfect, luminous object that symbolizes both the city's ancient maritime history, and its current attempts at modernization and progress. Measuring 15 meters in diameter, the crystal sphere is suspended over an open cylinder with a spiral ramp ascending the supporting walls. Visitors are taken by elevator to the heart of the sphere, a "secret courtyard" suspended over the water and dominated by the radial light source that illuminates the Pearl at night. When viewed from the interior, the spectacular, delicate web of the monument is immediately apparent. The structure of the sphere is defined by a pentagonal mesh, while the geometry of its glass surface is based on the dodecahedron. A series of polygonal superpositions creates a regular pattern in the form of an arabesque, so that each dodecahedron is composed of a central pentagon, five squares, and five triangular panels.

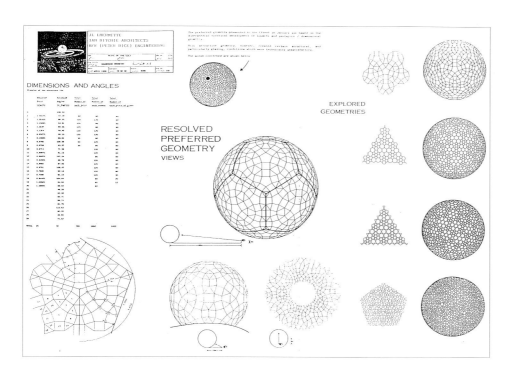

DIMENSIONS AND ANGLES

RESOLVED
PREFERRED
GEOMETRY
VIEWS

EXPLORED
GEOMETRIES

Opposite page: View of the model, with the arabesque web of the glass panels, and the central lighting system, which transforms the sphere into a beacon at night.

Top: Comparative table showing different geometrical solutions for the spherical surface. Center: View of the unfinished model. Bottom: Transverse section through the sphere and surrounding ramp and exhibition spaces.

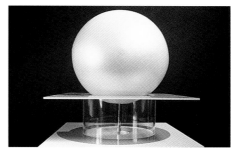

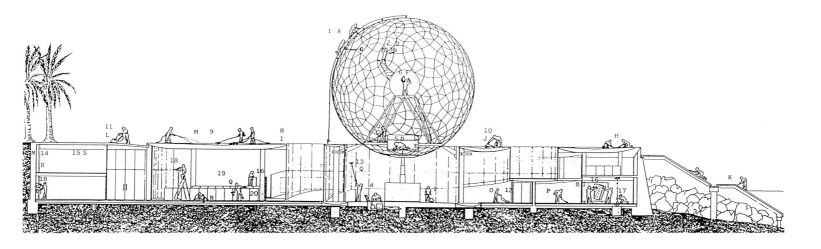

# New Meridian Planetarium, Greenwich

The Greenwich Meridian passes directly through the complex of buildings and astronomical observatories constructed between the 17th and 19th centuries, meeting the Thames approximately half a mile farther north.

The new planetarium, which overlooks the river, is located at this point, which is a short distance from Cutty Sark and the Royal Naval College.

The most important part of this new facility is its glass spheriscope, measuring 30 meters in diameter, whose equator is surrounded by a panoramic exhibition gallery. Constucted of a steel frame supporting both the inner and outer skins, its walls contain light sources that allow visitors to compose texts, images, and astronomical maps that can be viewed from the exterior through the panels of curved glass. Inside, on a suspended transparent glass floor, 300 spectators at a time are able to watch video projections that use the entire surface of the sphere as a screen.

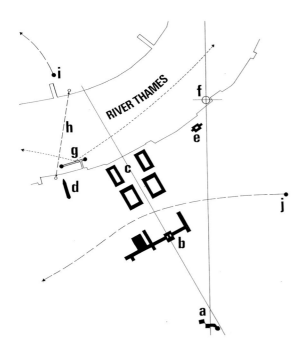

Top left: Location of the planetarium with respect to the celebrated classical architectural composition of the Greenwich waterfront. Top right: Perspective from the west. Bottom: East elevation.
Legend:
a  Royal Observatory
b  Queen's House and Maritime Museum
c  Royal Institute of Navigation
d  Cutty Sark
e  Trinity Hospital
f  Planetarium
g  Greenwich waterfront
h  Pedestrian tunnel
i  Underground station
j  Railway station

Opposite page: Transverse section of the planetarium looking west. The structure is made of stainless steel covered with a double layer of glass panels.

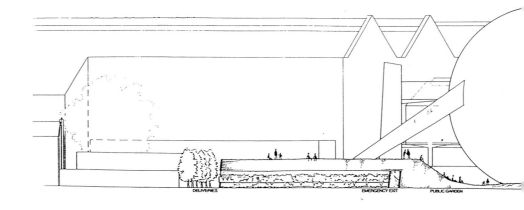

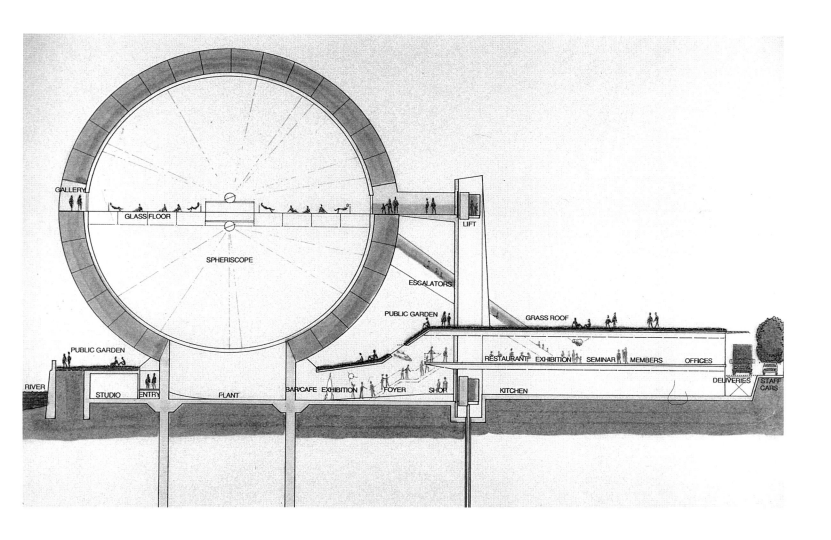

GALLERY

GLASS FLOOR

SPHERISCOPE

LIFT

ESCALATORS

PUBLIC GARDEN

GRASS ROOF

RESTAURANT   EXHIBITION   SEMINAR   MEMBERS   OFFICES

PUBLIC GARDEN

RIVER

STUDIO   ENTRY   PLANT   BAR/CAFE   EXHIBITION   FOYER   SHOP   KITCHEN   DELIVERIES   STAFF CARS

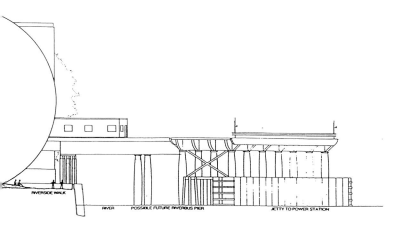

RIVERSIDE WALK

RIVER   POSSIBLE FUTURE RIVERBUS PIER   JETTY TO POWER STATION

# Ecology Gallery, Natural History Museum, London

**The Age of the Interactive Dinosaur.** In designing this project, Ritchie was faced with two major challenges. First, how to emphasize the importance of ecology in today's world, and the way in which architecture can be an effective means of communicating this message. Second, how to express the relationship between the linear, symmetrical order of the museum, with its structural elements and decorative motifs, and the form and function of the new gallery. After studying the various characteristics of the original building, which was designed by Alfred Waterhouse in 1873, Ritchie decided on a totally autonomous structure that could be easily dismantled and removed after a projected period of 10 years (1991-2001). Another major objective was finding a means to allow a closer look at the decorative details of the museum, which were placed at such a height that they were barely discernible. Today, as visitors walk through the gallery, they are able to view a series of exhibitions equipped with state-of-the-art technology. In keeping with the intent of Sir Richard Owen, the museum's founder, Ritchie has attempted to introduce the public at large to the latest advances in the natural sciences.

Waterhouse's original glass display cases, which he situated between the columns and walls of the museum, inspired Ritchie to design "thematic windows" that are large enough to contain not only the objects on exhibit, but the visitors as well. The glass walls, and the bridges that cross the chasm of the gallery, whose structural elements recall the basic elements of nature, create an asymmetrical spatial composition that reinforces the idea of a natural state of disequilibrium.

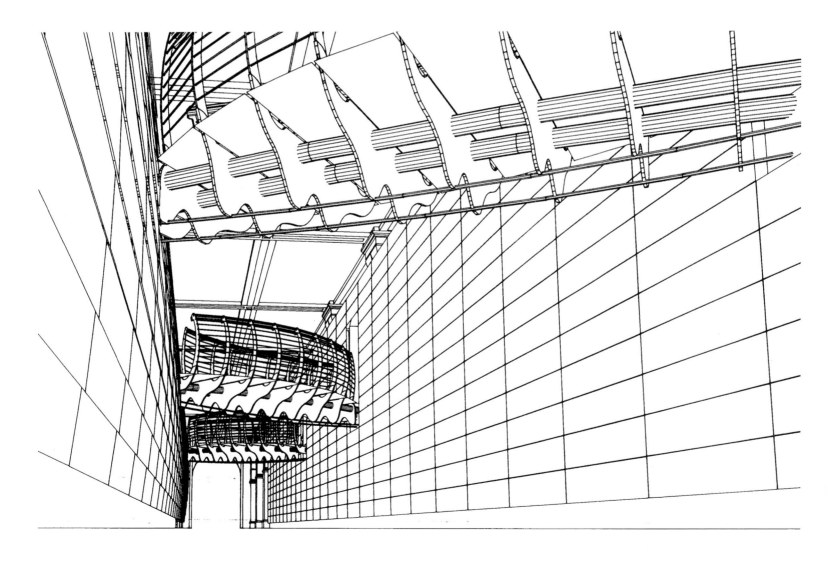

Opposite page: Perspective of the translucent walls and bridges.

Top and bottom: The gallery as seen from the atrium of the museum. Center: Plan of the upper level.

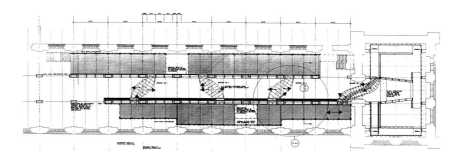

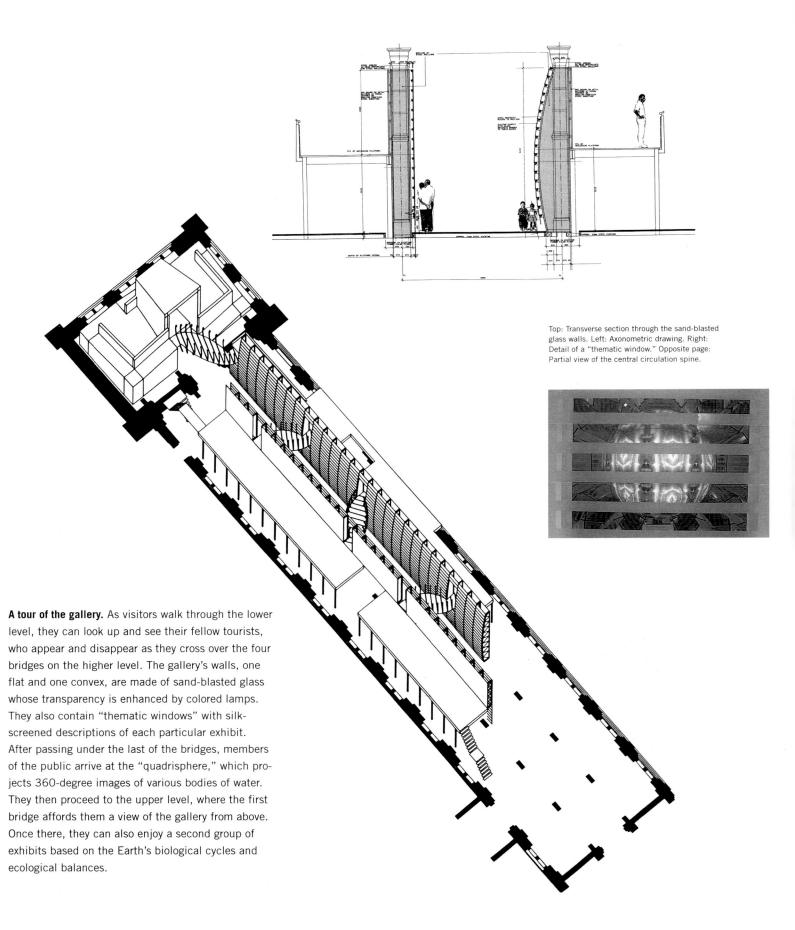

Top: Transverse section through the sand-blasted glass walls. Left: Axonometric drawing. Right: Detail of a "thematic window." Opposite page: Partial view of the central circulation spine.

**A tour of the gallery.** As visitors walk through the lower level, they can look up and see their fellow tourists, who appear and disappear as they cross over the four bridges on the higher level. The gallery's walls, one flat and one convex, are made of sand-blasted glass whose transparency is enhanced by colored lamps. They also contain "thematic windows" with silk-screened descriptions of each particular exhibit. After passing under the last of the bridges, members of the public arrive at the "quadrisphere," which projects 360-degree images of various bodies of water. They then proceed to the upper level, where the first bridge affords them a view of the gallery from above. Once there, they can also enjoy a second group of exhibits based on the Earth's biological cycles and ecological balances.

Left: Partial view of the gallery. Right: Detail section construction drawing.

Opposite page, top: Views of the entranceway. Center: Detail plan construction drawing of the museum sign indicating the way into the gallery. Bottom: Detail section construction drawings.

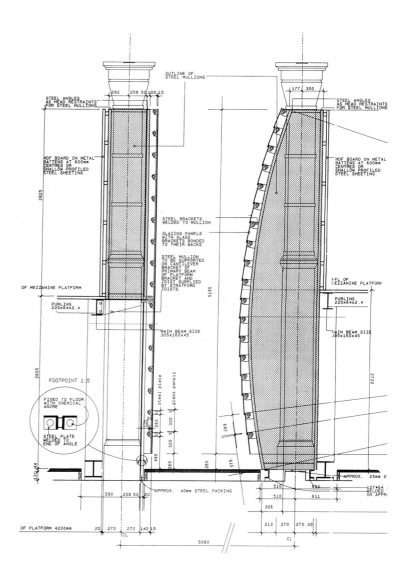

If you are thinking
sow seed.
If you are thinking
plant a tree.
If you are thinking
educate the people

Kuan Tzu Chinese
500 BC

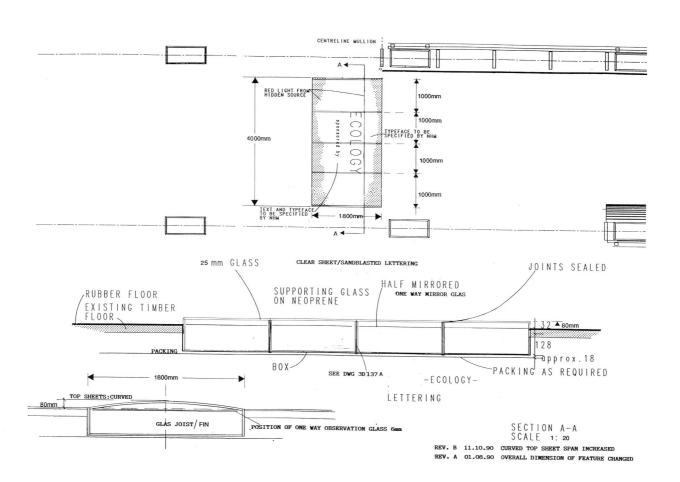

CENTRELINE MULLION

A

RED LIGHT FROM
HIDDEN SOURCE

1000mm

1000mm

ECOLOGY

sponsored by

4000mm

TYPEFACE TO BE
SPECIFIED BY NHM

1000mm

1000mm

TEXT AND TYPEFACE
TO BE SPECIFIED
BY NHM

1800mm

A

25 mm GLASS      CLEAR SHEET/SANDBLASTED LETTERING                    JOINTS SEALED

RUBBER FLOOR          SUPPORTING GLASS      HALF MIRRORED
EXISTING TIMBER       ON NEOPRENE           ONE WAY MIRROR GLAS
FLOOR                                                                    32   80mm

PACKING                                                                 128

BOX        SEE DWG 3D137 A                              approx.18
                                                      PACKING AS REQUIRED
                              —ECOLOGY—
                          LETTERING

1800mm

TOP SHEETS:CURVED

80mm

GLAS JOIST/FIN        POSITION OF ONE WAY OBSERVATION GLASS 6mm

SECTION A—A
SCALE 1:20

REV. B  11.10.90  CURVED TOP SHEET SPAN INCREASED
REV. A  01.08.90  OVERALL DIMENSION OF FEATURE CHANGED

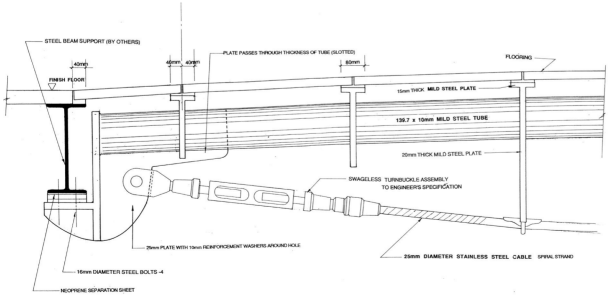

STEEL BEAM SUPPORT (BY OTHERS)

PLATE PASSES THROUGH THICKNESS OF TUBE (SLOTTED)

FLOORING

40mm

40mm  40mm

80mm

FINISH FLOOR

15mm THICK  MILD STEEL PLATE

139.7 x 10mm MILD STEEL TUBE

20mm THICK MILD STEEL PLATE

SWAGELESS  TURNBUCKLE ASSEMBLY
TO ENGINEER'S SPECIFICATION

25mm PLATE WITH 10mm REINFORCEMENT WASHERS AROUND HOLE

25mm  DIAMETER  STAINLESS  STEEL  CABLE  SPIRAL STRAND

16mm DIAMETER STEEL BOLTS -4

NEOPRENE SEPARATION SHEET

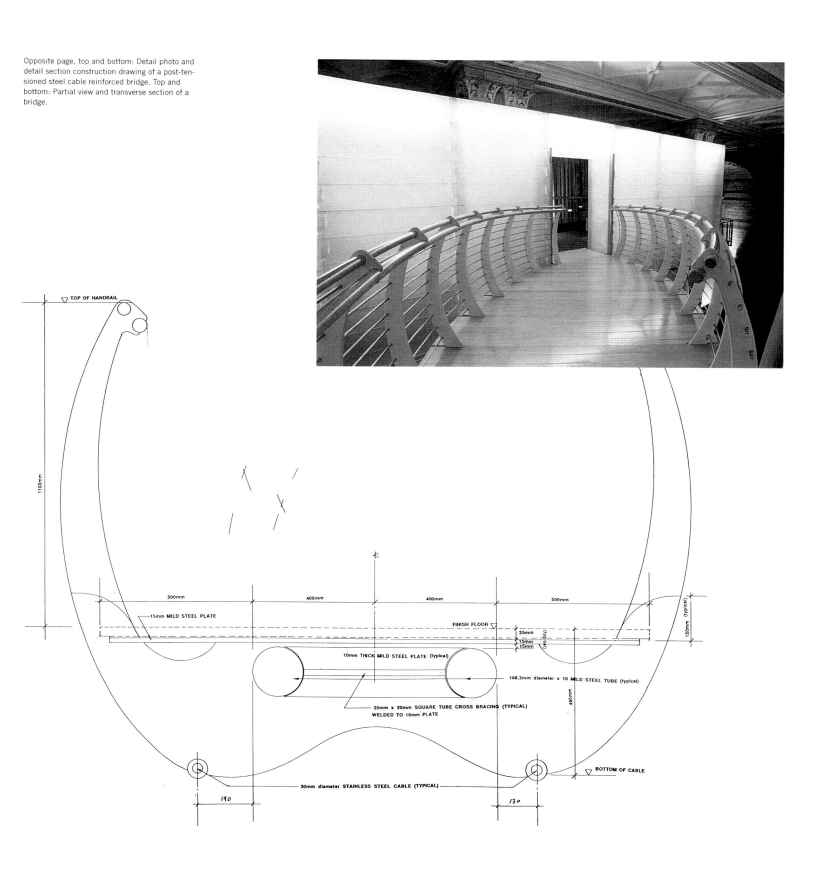

Opposite page, top and bottom: Detail photo and detail section construction drawing of a post-tensioned steel cable reinforced bridge. Top and bottom: Partial view and transverse section of a bridge.

▽ TOP OF HANDRAIL

1100mm

500mm    400mm    400mm    500mm

150mm (typical)

15mm MILD STEEL PLATE

FINISH FLOOR ▽

35mm (typical)
15mm
15mm

10mm THICK MILD STEEL PLATE (typical)

168.3mm diameter x 10 MILD STEEL TUBE (typical)

490mm

20mm x 20mm SQUARE TUBE CROSS BRACING (TYPICAL)
WELDED TO 10mm PLATE

▽ BOTTOM OF CABLE

30mm diameter STAINLESS STEEL CABLE (TYPICAL)

190    130

Above: Views of exhibits on the upper level. Left: Detail plan construction drawing of the side walls and bridge. Opposite page: Partial view of the quadrisphere.

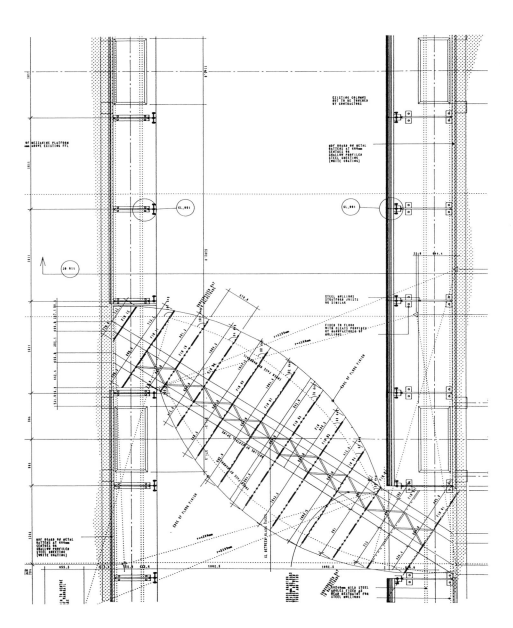

## Herne-Sodingen Academy, Emscher Park, Germany

At the heart of the proposed Herne-Sodingen project was an intellectual and moral commitment to education, both in terms of primary function (the Academy) and desire (ecology), which was to influence the architectural structure and physical interpretation of the park. Education was considered first and foremost the need to be aware, understand, and appreciate. In an ecological sense, this meant recognizing the beauty and value of different forms of life, and taking positive action to avoid the despoliation of the environment and the extinction of its inhabitants.

The reclamation of the landscape was the central theme of the authorities of the IBA Emscher Park region, as well as the primary objective of the Herne-Sodingen Academy Park. If high environmental expectations were to be met for the Academy, even more was expected of the landscape in which it was integrated.

Opposite page: Site plan. The park was traversed by a curved valley that began at the edge of Sodingen and proceeded in a southerly direction. This new topographical element, which was narrower in the area of the town, gradually opened up until it was literally absorbed by the surrounding landscape. The valley, which was the first clearing in the wood, and its pathway, which wound around Sodingen to the Volkspark in Herne, were reserved for pedestrians, cyclists, and emergency vehicles.

Below: View of the model. The forestation of the site involved primarily silver birches, which required the immediate control of pollutants filtering into the water table in order to survive. In an attempt to isolate the environment from the water table, vertical clay "walls," built into the ground, surrounded the wooded area.

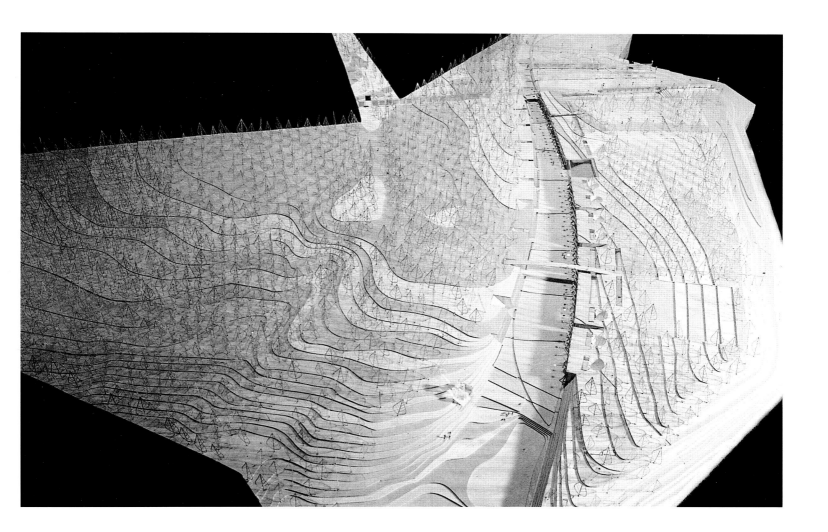

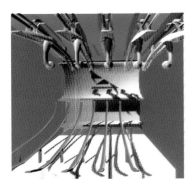

Designed to restore direct contact with nature, the landscape, which was to provide much more than simple visual pleasure, would fulfill a number of important functions, including the introduction of new ways to use materials, energy sources, and manpower. This approach was based primarily on the need to reestablish a natural equilibrium in an environment that had long suffered the devastating effects of industrial pollution.

Promoting a heightened social awareness of the importance of environmental change was to be accomplished by encouraging respect for the ecological principles involved in the management and administration of open spaces, and by training future planners and designers. The educational opportunities offered by this site were meant to play a significant role in helping individuals to understand fully the concept of natural landscape restoration, which in turn would act as a catalyst for further development of the park.

**The woods and the valley.** Herne-Sodingen Academy Park was planned as a wooded area available not only to the Academy, but to all sectors of the surrounding community as well.

In the space of only a few decades, the primary means by which barren ground was colonized by new plant regimes would reflect the entire history of the natural evolution of a landscape that had been transformed into a mature woodland area. Successful implementation of this project required the active participation of the regional authorities, townspeople, and local youth, in terms of their knowledge and awareness of the procedures used, and the amount of time involved.

In addition to the Academy's regular courses, the park hoped to provide learning opportunities that were both formal, such as the study of the soil and natural habitat, and informal, such as children's play. The most important part of the educational component was the actual transformation of the site, and its proper utilization over the course of time, which would serve to create confidence and pride in the future.

The overall architectural plan, which was designed to encourage a reassessment of attitudes toward the future, was firmly based on an awareness of the social and political context of Sodingen. The idea of an educational woodland park, which was inspired by a need to understand and appreciate the immediate environment, involved three key components: its physical characteristics and interrelationships, its surrounding social structure, and the memories it evoked.

Although the park was relatively flat, it was higher than the surrounding territory to the west and northwest. The natural process of forestation involved planting silver birches in isolated pockets of the landscape. Contaminants were to be removed by either natural or artificial means, as the park's geometric structure precluded construction in certain areas, at least at the initial stage. The water table, which was several meters below the surface, had absorbed pollutants washed through by rainfall. Above the water table, the soil still contained considerable amounts of mineral waste from demolished buildings and mining activities. Methane gas was also being released from the ground, primarily through controlled vents above the three vertical shafts.

Opposite page: Perspective of the valley.

Above: Computer generated interior perspective
of an apartment in the proposed residential unit
for students.

There were no buildings planned within the park, only surfaces and topology. The principal structural elements of the Academy, which was to be located within the valley, created "built banks," or sides. The east side, a "glass cascade," housed the educational facilities, while the west side, a covered walk, provided student dormitories. Together, the two sides formed the "banks" of a stream that meandered through the valley. As visitors entered the park, their first view would be of the landscape itself. Not until they began to descend the valley would they discover the Academy.

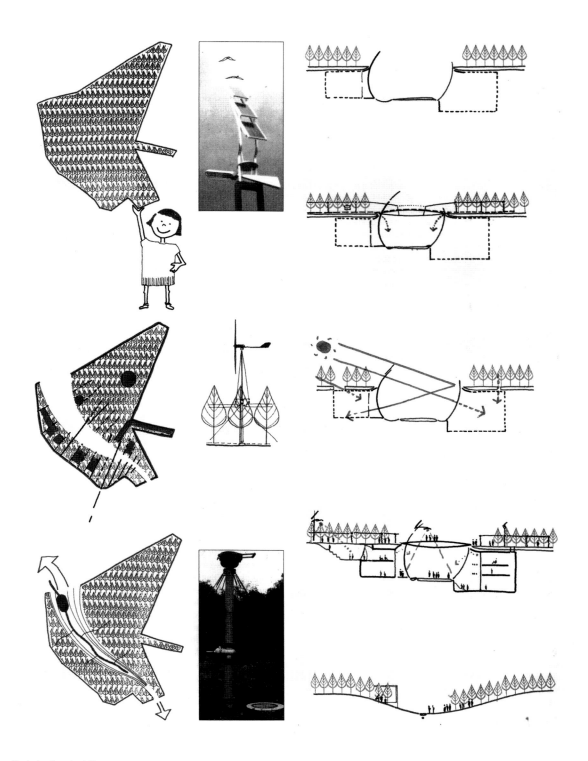

Clockwise, from top left:
Perimeter of the park (block diagram)
Solar energy generator (photo)
"Built banks," showing student housing sites
(2 sketches)
Sketch illustrating the valley's exposure to sunlight
Public and private domains (two sketches)

Methane gas extractor (photo)
Stream meandering through the valley
(block diagram)
"Clearing" in the silver birch woods
(block diagram)
Wind-driven water pump (center sketch)

Top left and right: Designs by Andy Goldsworthy and Walter De Maria. Bottom: Concept diagrams of the Academy, showing the linear nature of the valley, pedestrian and vehicular access routes, and overall landscape design.

The Academy Park was spatially defined by two series of "radiating walls," one of which emanated from the countryside, and the other from the heart of Sodingen. Some of these walls were single lines, while others were "doubled," or twinned. Conceived of as "sculptures" within the woodland, they were to be designed by artists such as Richard Long, Walter De Maria, Michael Heizer, and Robert Irwin.

In reality, the walls were a light framework providing support for various functions, such as storage areas, bridge walls, raised walkways, and retaining walls, and delineating various activity areas within the park.

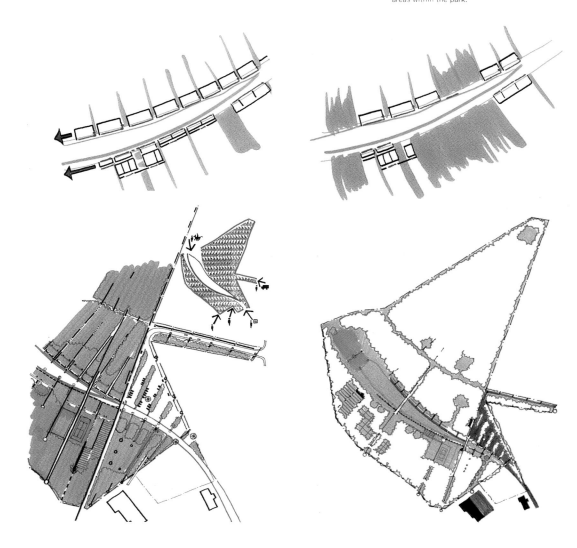

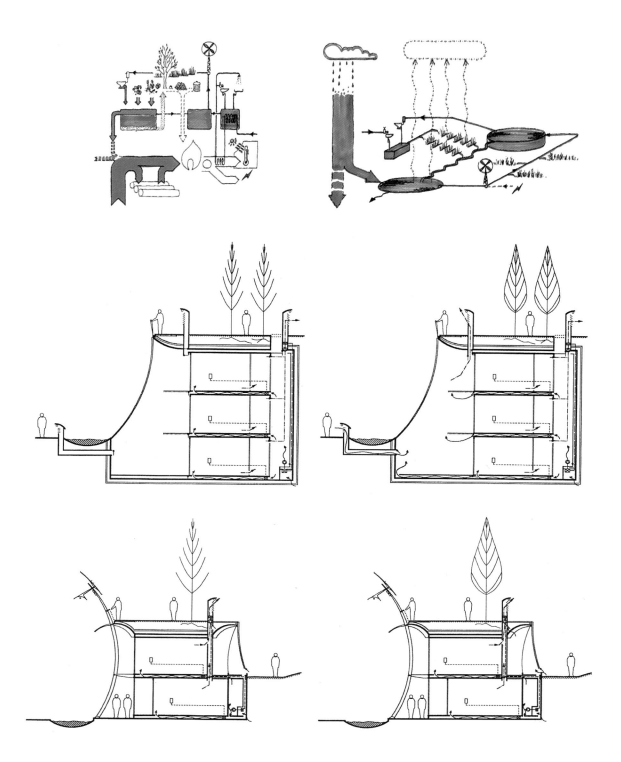

Top: Site energy sources and recycling: Methane gas, solar energy, wind, and biomass were to be used to provide energy for the Academy. Excess stored methane was transferred locally to provide energy to nearby buildings. Site water sources and recycling: The new valley landscape allowed for the collection of water from the site and its build-ings through the use of wind-driven pumps, water storage, solar energy storage, and filtration beds. Center: Transverse sections showing air-flow in winter and summer. The student dormitories were prefabricated units connected by a continu-ous glass panel.

Bottom: Floors and ceilings were separated by an air-void that was used as a combined surface-air heating system. The seminar rooms of the Academy on the upper floor were closed off to the north by a thermally insulated external wall, and to the south by a glazed buffer zone. Below the seminar rooms were the administrative offices.

## Open-Air Concert Platform, Crystal Palace Park, London

The name Crystal Palace evokes memories of one of the most extraordinary buildings ever attempted. By the end of the last century, the park surrounding Joseph Paxton's pavilion had already become the scene of an annual series of public concerts, which enjoyed enormous popularity for decades. The Bromley Borough Council decided to revive this tradition by commissioning a permanent open-air concert platform on the site of, and in the spirit of, the Crystal Palace that once stood there.

The most crucial aspect of this project was the visual relationship between the beauty of the landscape and the platform's structural design. As the central element in a wooded area with a small pond, the platform is intended to reinforce, rather than alter, the sense of spatial unity. By making the landscape his primary objective, Ritchie was able to identify the following design criteria:

Color: The traditional neo-classical structures built for English parks retained the natural whiteness of their original stone. During the Victorian era, such constructions were made of cast iron painted gray, green, and white. However, as white is not naturally compatible with the landscape in that it introduces too strong a contrast with the surrounding environment and immediately attracts the eye, Ritchie chose to utilize basic earth tones and the changing reflections of the water in the pond as his color palette.

*Gravitas* and *levitas:* English neo-classical parkland buildings have always emphasized the principle of *gravitas,* both in their solid relationship with the ground and materiality of their architecture. Victorian pavilions (more Gothic than classical) have stressed instead the quality of lightness.

The open-air platform at Crystal Park attempts to express both *gravitas,* through the weight of the struc-

ture itself, and *levitas,* through the manner in which it relates to the landscape setting.

Complexity and simplicity: Inasmuch as it attempts to reflect the natural surroundings, the English park is generally rather complex. In keeping with much of contemporary architecture, especially in Europe, which has become increasingly simple and geometric, the minimalist nature of the concert platform (simplicity) has been designed as more landscape than building (complexity).

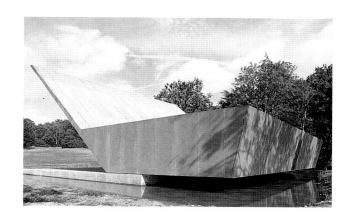

Top and left: Views of the platform. Below: Study sketches illustrating the main design elements: the stone base, Corten steel structure, open area for public facilities, and protective canopy.

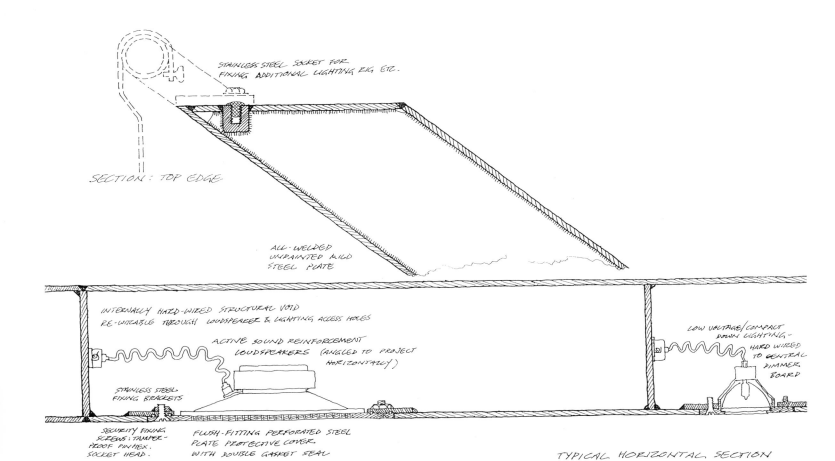

STAINLESS STEEL SOCKET FOR
FIXING ADDITIONAL LIGHTING RIG ETC.

SECTION: TOP EDGE

ALL-WELDED
UNPAINTED MILD
STEEL PLATE

INTERNALLY HARD-WIRED STRUCTURAL VOID
RE-WIRABLE THROUGH LOUDSPEAKER & LIGHTING ACCESS HOLES

ACTIVE SOUND REINFORCEMENT
LOUDSPEAKERS (ANGLED TO PROJECT
HORIZONTALLY)

LOW VOLTAGE/COMPACT
DOWN LIGHTING -
HARD WIRED
TO CENTRAL
DIMMER
BOARD

STAINLESS STEEL
FIXING BRACKETS

SECURITY FIXING
SCREWS: TAMPER-
PROOF PIN HEX.
SOCKET HEAD.

FLUSH-FITTING PERFORATED STEEL
PLATE PROTECTIVE COVER
WITH DOUBLE GASKET SEAL

TYPICAL HORIZONTAL SECTION

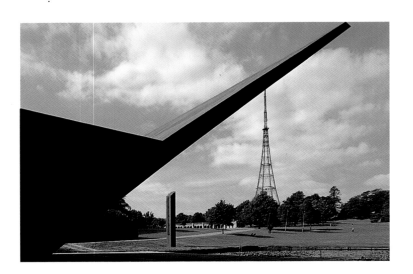

Top: Detail section of top edge of canopy. Center:
Longitudinal section through top of canopy,
including the series of structural voids containing
lighting projectors. Bottom: View from northeast.

Opposite page: View from southwest, showing
the platform overlooking the small pond. The
slight incline of the clearing forms a natural
amphitheater.

90

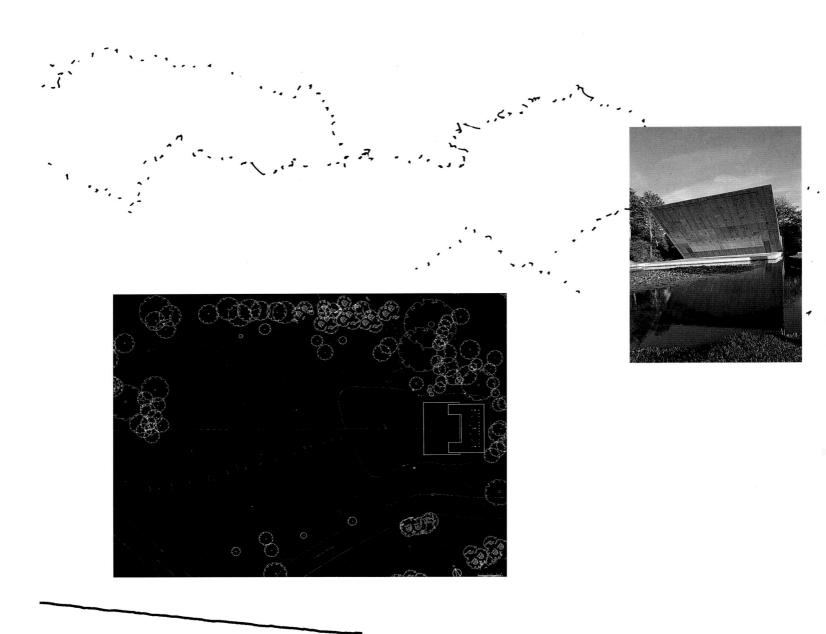

Opposite page: Top: Images of the construction site. Center: View looking east at canopy. Bottom: Site plan with topographical contour lines.

Top: Transverse section of platform and plan of canopied pavilion. Bottom: Concept drawing.

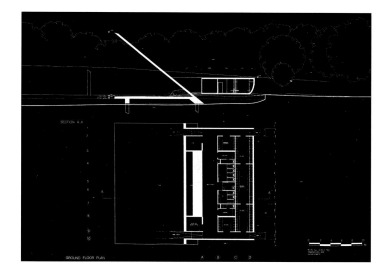

## Autobiographical Notes

I began studying architecture in Liverpool, where I spent most of my time with poets such as Roger McGough (more or less the English equivalent of Jacques Prévert). After this I worked in Germany, and then in Oito, Japan. Although I was not particularly interested in architecture at the time, I was struck by certain buildings designed by Arata Isozaki (whom I only learned about many years later).

When I returned to England, I enrolled in the Westminster Planning School of London, which I graduated from in 1972. For my final dissertation, I chose Richard Rogers as my advisor, but as he considered my thesis too philosophical and abstract, I turned to Warren Chalk, a member of the Archigram movement, with whose encouragement, more than help, I produced an audio-visual display on future land use for leisure-time activities in an urban environment. I also started collaborating with Jocelyne Van den Bossche, who was to become my life-long companion.

At that time, the Archigram group, which had won the Monte Carlo competition, seemed very interested in my ideas. Through Warren Chalk, I was introduced to Peter Cook and Ron Herron, with whom, like Richard Rogers, I would develop lasting professional relationships. Robert Maxwell, who was not a member of my dissertation committee, was selected to hear me defend my thesis. Unbeknownst to me, Maxwell, who would later become dean of the School of Architecture at Princeton University, recommended me to Norman Foster. This was how Jocelyne and I began working for the architectural firm of Foster and Michael Hopkins, who were partners at the time. I was immediately assigned to the Willis, Faber & Dumas office building project in Ipswich, where I made friends with two of Foster's consultants, Anthony Hunt and Martin Francis. During the course of the project, I also had occasion to work with Jean Prouvé, who, together with Francis, taught me the importance of technical competence and strict methodology, both of which he approached with the greatest humility.

Peter Rice, who had just been invited to collaborate on the Park Galleries project for the new National Museum of Science and Technology that Adrien Fainsilber was designing for Paris's La Villette Park, then asked me if I wanted to work with him. I accepted his offer, and also suggested that he get in touch with Martin Francis, an expert in the field of industrial design who was building yachts in France. Although Peter was not particularly enthusiastic about the steel structure of Fainsilber's new building, he was interested in studying the properties and possibilities of its glass walls. In 1981, during a dinner in a Parisian restaurant, the three of us decided to open a technical design studio known as Rice Francis Ritchie, or "RFR." As I was only 34 at the time—much younger than my colleagues—I was very grateful to Peter for making me an equal partner.

Our first associate, Henry Beardsley, a structural engineer who had been part of Peter's team at the Centre Pompidou and a member of the design studio formed by Peter and Renzo Piano, was soon followed by Hugh Dutton, who had recently graduated from the Architectural Association School of London and begun working for my firm.

For five years, I divided my time equally between London and Paris. RFR, which completed the greenhouses at La Villette in 1986, had also created an entirely new team approach that put engineers, architects, and industrial designers on an equal—-and harmonious—footing. My 10-year association with Peter Rice was the equivalent of a university course in applied structural engineering. We were also the closest of friends, and through him I was able to establish an important working relationship, which is still going on today, with the engineering firm of Ove Arup.

*Ian Ritchie*

**Pearl of the Gulf, Dubai, 1988**
Ian Ritchie *with* Jean-Louis Lhermitte
*structures* Peter Rice
*geometric views* Ensor Holiday, Keith Lewis

**B8 Building, Stockley Park, Heathrow, 1988-89**
Ian Ritchie Architects
Bjørn Bergfeld, Simon Connolly, Brigitte Desrochers, Dominique Gagnon, David Kahn, Ian Montgomerie, Ornat O'Brien, Ian Ritchie, Anthony Summers, Edmund Wan, Jude Welsby
*structures* Ove Arup & Partners

**Vertical Circulation Towers, Reina Sofia Museum of Modern Art, Madrid, 1989-91**
Ian Ritchie Architects
*with* Simon Connolly, in association with J.I. Ihiguez & A. Vasquez
*collaborator* Jon Buck
*structures* John Thornton and Bruce Gibbons (Ove Arup & Partners)

**Bermondsey Station, Jubilee Line Extension, London, 1989-98**
Ian Ritchie Architects
John Comparelli, James de Soyres, Mark Innes, Toke Kharmpej, Ian Montgomerie, Henning Rambow, Ian Ritchie, Anthony Summers, Paul Simovic, Gordon Talbot
*structures* Ove Arup & Partners

**Ecology Gallery, Natural History Museum, London, 1989-91**
Ian Ritchie Architects
*with* K. Schnetkamp, Henning Rambow, R. Kroeker, Ian Ritchie
*structures* Peter Rice (Ove Arup & Partners)

**New Meridian Planetarium, Greenwich, England, 1991**
Ian Ritchie Architects
Ian Ritchie, Simon Connolly
*structures* Ove Arup & Partners

**Herne-Sodingen Academy, Emscher Park, Germany, 1991**
Ian Ritchie Architects
Ian Ritchie, Simon Connolly, Gurjit Suri, Henning Rambow, Bruno Duchet
*structures* Neil Thomas (Atelier One)
*landscape* Charles Funke Associates

**Experimental Greenhouse, Terrasson-Lavilledieu, Dordogne, France, 1992-94**
Ian Ritchie Architects *with* Simon Connolly, Edmund Wan
*structures* John Thornton, John Berry (Ove Arup & Partners)
*park design* Kathryn Gustafson (Paysage-Land)

**Main Hall, International Exhibition Center, Leipzig, Germany, 1992-96**
Ian Ritchie Architects
Ian Ritchie, Simon Connolly, Henning Rambow, Anthony Summers, Elden Croy, John Randle
*structures* Ipp, Ove Arup & Partners
*overall fairground design* Von Gerkan, Marg & Partners

**Royal Albert Dock Rowing Club and Boathouse, London, 1993-98**
Ian Ritchie Architects
Anthony Summers, Ian Ritchie, Clarissa Matthews, Stephen Quinn, Robert Thum
*with* Ove Arup & Partners, Davis, Langdon & Everest

**Tower Bridge Theatre, London, 1995**
Ian Ritchie Architects
Ian Ritchie, Simon Connolly, Anthony Summers, Robert Thum, Toby Edward
*with* John Lovell, Chris Pembridge, Chris Jofeh, Mike Bevan (Ove Arup & Partners)
*acoustics* Raf Orlowski, Derek Sugden (Ove Arup & Partners)

**Open-Air Concert Platform, Crystal Palace Park, London, 1996-97**
Ian Ritchie Architects
Ian Ritchie, Simon Connolly, Helgo von Meier
*structures* Neil Thomas (Atelier One)
*acoustics* Paul Gillieron

Photographs by Jocelyne Van den Bossche

Printed and bound in Italy
by Arti Grafiche Motta, Milan